A Season's Tale

Thirty five knitting designs
for men, women and children

Kim Hargreaves

ROWAN

Designs & Styling Kim Hargreaves
Photographer Joey Toller
Hair & Make-up Annabelle Hobbs
Book Design Kim Hargreaves
Design Co-ordinator Kathleen Hargreaves
Design Layout Les Dunford
Knitting co-ordinators Elizabeth Armitage & Lyndsay Kaye
Pattern writers Stella Smith, Sue Whiting & Tricia McKenzie

British Library Cataloguing in Publication Data
Rowan Yarns
A Season's Tale
1. Knitting - patterns
1 Title
ISBN 0-9525375-4

Printed by KHL Printing Co Pte Ltd
Singapore

Contents

RUTH

YARN
Rowan Rowanspun DK

	S	
To fit bust	86	cm
	34	in
	7	x 50gm

(photographed in Rush 737)

NEEDLES
1 pair 3¾mm (no 9) (US 5) needles
1 pair 4mm (no 8) (US 6) needles

STUD FASTENERS - 6

TENSION
22 sts and 32 rows to 10 cm measured over herringbone pattern using 4mm (US 6) needles.

Pattern note: Increases for pattern (but NOT shaping) are worked as folls: place point of right needle behind left needle, insert needle point from the top down through the purled head of st below next st on left needle, knit this st then knit the stitch above. When working shapings in this pattern, take care not to work the pattern inc unless you are able to work corresponding K2tog.

BACK
Cast on 99 sts using 3¾mm (US 5) needles.
Purl 1 row.
Now work in herringbone patt from chart (see page 84) as folls:
Row 1 (RS): *K2tog, K2, inc in next st (see pattern note), K2, rep from * to last st, K1.
Row 2: Purl.
Row 3: K1, *K2, inc in next st (see pattern note), K2, K2tog, rep from * to end.
Row 4: Purl.
These 4 rows form herringbone patt and are repeated throughout.
Patt a further 4 rows.
Change to 4mm (US 6) needles.
Work a further 6 rows, ending with a WS row.
Dec 1 st at each end of next and every foll 6th row to 87 sts, then on every foll 4th row until 83 sts rem.
Work 9 rows.
Inc 1 st at each end of next and every foll 8th row to 91 sts, then on every foll 6th row until there are 99 sts, taking inc sts into patt.
Cont straight until chart row 122 has been completed. Work measures approx. 38 cm, ending with a WS row.
Shape armholes
Keeping patt correct, cast off 4 sts at beg of next 2 rows. 91 sts.
Dec 1 st at each end of next 3 rows, then on foll 5 alt rows, then on every foll 4th row until 71 sts rem.
Cont straight until chart row 186 has been completed. Armhole measures approx. 20 cm, ending with a WS row.
Shape shoulders and back neck
Keeping patt correct, cast off 6 sts at beg of next 2 rows. 59 sts.
Next row (RS): Cast off 6 sts, patt until there are 10 (10: 11: 11: 10) sts on right needle and turn, leaving rem sts on a holder.
Work each side of neck separately.

Cast off 4 sts at beg of next row.
Cast off rem 6 sts.
With RS facing, rejoin yarn to rem sts, cast off centre 27 sts, patt to end.
Work to match first side, reversing shapings.

LEFT FRONT
Cast on 57 sts using 3¾mm (US 5) needles.
Purl 1 row.
Now work in herringbone patt from chart as folls:
Row 1 (RS): *K2tog, K2, inc in next st, K2, rep from * to last st, K1.
Row 2: Purl.
Row 3: K1, *K2, inc in next st, K2, K2tog, rep from * to end.
Row 4: Purl.
These 4 rows form herringbone patt and are repeated throughout.
Patt a further 4 rows.
Change to 4mm (US 6) needles.
Work a further 6 rows, ending with a WS row.
Dec 1 st at beg of next and every foll 6th row to 51 sts, then on every foll 4th row until 49 sts rem.
Work 9 rows.
Inc 1 st at beg of next and every foll 8th row to 53 sts, then on every foll 6th row until there are 57 sts, taking inc sts into patt.
Cont straight until left front matches back to beg of armhole shaping, ending with a WS row.
Shape armhole
Keeping patt correct, cast off 4 sts at beg of next row. 53 sts.
Work 1 row.
Dec 1 st at armhole edge of next 3 rows, then on foll 5 alt rows, then on every foll 4th row until 43 sts rem.
Cont straight until 23 rows less have been worked than on back to start of shoulder shaping, ending with a RS row.
Shape neck
Keeping patt correct, cast off 16 sts at beg of next row. 27 sts.
Dec 1 st at neck edge on next 5 rows, then on foll 2 alt rows, then on every foll 4th row until 18 sts rem.
Work 5 rows, ending with a WS row.
Shape shoulder
Keeping patt correct, cast off 6 sts at beg of next and foll alt row.
Work 1 row. Cast off rem 6 sts.

RIGHT FRONT
Cast on 57 sts using 3¾mm (US 5) needles.
Purl 1 row.
Now work in herringbone patt as folls:
Row 1 (RS): *K2tog, K2, inc in next st, K2, rep from * to last st, K1.
Row 2: Purl.
Row 3: K1, *K2, inc in next st, K2, K2tog, rep from * to end.
Row 4: Purl.
These 4 rows form herringbone patt and are repeated throughout.
Patt a further 4 rows.
Change to 4mm (US 6) needles.
Work a further 6 rows, ending with a WS row.
Dec 1 st at end of next and every foll 6th row to 51 sts, then on every foll 4th row until 49 sts rem.
Complete to match left front, reversing shapings.

SLEEVES (both alike)
Cast on 50 sts using 3¾mm (US 5) needles.
Purl 1 row.
Now work in herringbone patt from chart as folls:
Row 1 (RS): *K2tog, K2, inc in next st, K2, rep from * to last st, K1.
Row 2: Purl.
Row 3: K1, *K2, inc in next st, K2, K2tog, rep from * to end.
Row 4: Purl.
These 4 rows form herringbone patt and are repeated throughout.
Patt a further 6 rows.
Change to 4mm (US 6) needles.
Cont in patt, inc 1 st at each end of next and every foll 10th row to 70 sts, then on every foll 8th row until there are 76 sts, taking inc sts into patt.
Cont straight until chart row 138 has been completed. Sleeve measures approx. 43 cm.
Shape top
Keeping patt correct, cast off 4 sts at beg of next 2 rows. 68 sts.
Dec 1 st at each end of next 3 rows, then on foll 3 alt rows, then on every foll 4th row until 48 sts rem.
Work 1 row, ending with a WS row.
Dec 1 st at each end of next and foll alt row, then on foll 5 rows. 34 sts.
Cast off 3 sts at beg of next 2 rows, then 6 sts at beg of foll 2 rows.
Cast off rem 16 sts.

(Knitting instructions continued on page 82)

45 cm (17.5 in)

58 cm (23 in)

43 cm (17 in)

LOCHGELLY

YARN
Rowan Rowanspun Chunky

	XS	S	M	L	XL
To fit bust	81	86	91	97	102cm
	32	34	36	38	40 in
	20	20	21	22	23 x 100gm

(photographed in Cardamom 983)

NEEDLES
1 pair 8mm (no 0) (US 11) needles
1 pair 9mm (no 00) (US 13) needles
1 pair 10mm (no 000) (US 15) needles

BUTTONS - 5

TENSION
16 sts and 20 rows to 10 cm measured over pattern using 10mm (US 15) needles.

BACK
Cast on 89 (93: 97: 101: 105) sts using 9mm (US 13) needles.
Row 1 (RS): K1, *slip next st with yarn at back (WS) of work, K1, rep from * to end.
Row 2: K1, *P1, K1, rep from * to end.
These 2 rows form patt.
Work in patt for a further 18 rows, ending with a WS row.
Change to 10mm (US 15) needles. Cont straight until back measures 99 cm, ending with a WS row.
Shape armholes
Keeping patt correct, cast off 4 sts at beg of next 2 rows. 81 (85: 89: 93: 97) sts.
Next row (RS) (dec): Patt 4 sts, K3tog, patt to last 7 sts, K3tog tbl, patt 4 sts.
Work 3 rows.
Rep last 4 rows twice more and then first of these rows (the dec row) again. 65 (69: 73: 77: 81) sts.
Cont straight until armhole measures 28 (28: 29: 29: 30) cm, ending with a WS row.
Shape shoulders and back neck
Keeping patt correct, cast off 7 (7: 8: 8: 9) sts at beg of next 2 rows. 51 (55: 57: 61: 63) sts.
Next row (RS): Cast off 7 (7: 8: 8: 9) sts, patt until there are 10 (11: 11: 12: 12) sts on right needle and turn, leaving rem sts on a holder.
Work each side of neck separately.
Cast off 4 sts at beg of next row.
Cast off rem 6 (7: 7: 8: 8) sts.
With RS facing, rejoin yarn to rem sts, cast off centre 17 (19: 19: 21: 21) sts, patt to end.
Work to match first side, reversing shapings.

POCKET LININGS (make 2)
Cast on 23 (23: 23: 25: 25) sts using 10mm (US 15) needles.
Work in patt as given for back for 18 cm, ending with a WS row. Break yarn and leave sts on a holder.

LEFT FRONT
Cast on 49 (51: 53: 55: 57) sts using 9mm (US 13) needles.
Work in patt as given for back for 20 rows, ending with a WS row.
Change to 10mm (US 15) needles.
Cont straight until left front measures 71 cm, ending with a WS row.
Place pocket
Next row (RS): Patt 6 (8: 10: 10: 12) sts, slip next 23 (23: 23: 25: 25) sts onto a holder and, in their place, patt across 23 (23: 23: 25: 25) sts of first pocket lining, patt to end.
Cont straight until left front matches back to beg of armhole shaping, ending with a WS row.
Shape armhole
Keeping patt correct, cast off 4 sts at beg of next row. 45 (47: 49: 51: 53) sts.
Work 1 row.
Next row (RS) (dec): Patt 4 sts, K3tog, patt to end.
Work 3 rows.
Rep last 4 rows twice more and then first of these rows (the dec row) again. 37 (39: 41: 43: 45) sts.
Cont straight until 14 rows less have been worked than on back to start of shoulder shaping, ending with a WS row.
Shape neck
Next row (RS): Patt 26 (27: 29: 30: 32) sts and turn, leaving rem 11 (12: 12: 13: 13) sts on a holder.
Work 1 row.
Next row (RS) (dec): Patt to last 6 (7: 7: 6: 6) sts, K3tog tbl, patt 3 (4: 4: 3: 3) sts.
Rep last 2 rows twice more. 20 (21: 23: 24: 26) sts.
Work 7 rows, ending with a WS row.
Shape shoulder
Keeping patt correct, cast off 7 (7: 8: 8: 9) sts at beg of next and foll alt row.
Work 1 row. Cast off rem 6 (7: 7: 8: 8) sts.
Mark positions for 5 buttons along left front opening edge – lowest button to be 50 cm up from cast-on edge, top button to be 5 cm down from neck shaping and rem 3 buttons evenly spaced between.

RIGHT FRONT
Cast on 49 (51: 53: 55: 57) sts using 9mm (US 13) needles.
Work in patt as given for back for 20 rows, ending with a WS row.
Change to 10mm (US 15) needles.
Cont straight until right front measures 50 cm, end with a WS row.
Next row (buttonhole row) (RS): Patt 4 sts, yfwd (to make a buttonhole), K2tog, patt to end.
Making a further 4 buttonholes in this way and noting that no further reference will be made to buttonholes, cont straight until right front measures 71 cm, ending with a WS row.
Place pocket
Next row (RS): Patt 20 sts, slip next 23 (23: 23: 25: 25) sts onto a holder and, in their place, patt across 23 (23: 23: 25: 25) sts of second pocket lining, patt to end.
Complete to match left front, reversing shapings.

SLEEVES (both alike)
Cast on 61 (61: 63: 65: 65) sts using 10mm (US 15) needles. Beg with row 1, work in patt as given for back as folls:
Dec 1 st at each end of 5th and every foll 6th row until 53 (53: 55: 57: 57) sts rem.
Work 1 row, ending with a WS row.
Change to 9mm (US 13) needles. Inc 1 st at each end of 5th and every foll 6th row until there are 59 (59: 61: 63: 63) sts, taking inc sts into patt.
Work 5 rows, ending with a WS row.
Change to 10mm (US 15) needles. Inc 1 st at each end of next and every foll 4th row until there are 89 (89: 93: 93: 95) sts, taking inc sts into patt.
Cont straight until sleeve measures 58 (58: 59: 59: 59) cm, ending with a WS row.
Shape top
Keeping patt correct, cast off 4 sts at beg of next 2 rows. 81 (81: 85: 85: 87) sts.
Work 2 rows.
Next row (RS) (dec): Patt 4 (4: 3: 4: 3) sts, K3tog, patt to last 7 (7: 6: 7: 6) sts, K3tog tbl, patt 4 (4: 3: 4: 3) sts.
Work 3 rows. Rep last 4 rows twice more.
Cast off rem 69 (69: 73: 73: 75) sts.

MAKING UP
PRESS all pieces as described on the info page.
Join shoulder seams using back stitch, or mattress stitch if preferred.
Collar
With RS facing and 8mm (US 11) needles, slip 11 (12: 12: 13: 13) sts from right front holder onto right needle, rejoin yarn and pick up and knit 10 sts up right side of neck, 19 (21: 21: 23: 23) sts from back, and 10 sts down left side of neck, then patt across 11 (12: 12: 13: 13) sts from left front holder. 61 (65: 65: 69: 69) sts.
Cont in patt as set by front opening edge sts until collar measures 10 cm.
Cast off firmly in patt.
Pocket tops (both alike)
Slip 23 (23: 23: 25: 25) sts from pocket holder onto 9mm (US 13) needles and rejoin yarn with RS facing.
Work in patt as set for 2 rows. Cast off in patt.
See information page for finishing instructions, setting in sleeves using the shallow set-in method.
Leave side seams open for first 50 cm for side vents and reverse sleeve seams for first 15 cm for turn-back. Fold 12 cm cuff to RS.

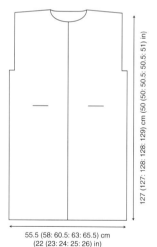

127 (127: 128: 128: 129) cm (50 (50: 50.5: 50.5: 51) in)

55.5 (58: 60.5: 63: 65.5) cm (22 (23: 24: 25: 26) in)

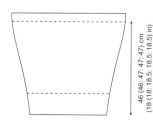

46 (46: 47: 47: 47) cm (18 (18: 18.5: 18.5: 18.5) in)

Opposite: Cameron Sweater knitted in Rowanspun Aran, knitting instructions on page 8 & Lochgelly Coat knitted in Rowanspun Chunky

CAMERON

YARN

Rowan Rowanspun Aran or Rowanspun DK

To fit age	4-5	6-7	8-9	10-11	12-13	years

Rowan Rowanspun Aran

Laced neck	4	5	5	6	6 x 100gm
Crew neck	4	4	5	5	6 x 100gm

Rowan Rowanspun DK★

Laced neck	8	9	10	11	12 x 50gm
Crew neck	7	8	9	10	11 x 50gm

(laced neck sweater photographed in Rowanspun DK in Eau de Nil 735)

	ladies			mens		
	S	M	L	M	L	XL
To fit bust/chest	86	91	97	102	107	112	cm
	34	36	38	40	42	44	in

Rowan Rowanspun Aran

Laced neck	7	7	8	8	9	9 x100gm
Crew neck	7	7	7	8	8	8 x100gm

Rowan Rowanspun DK★

Laced neck	13	14	15	16	16	17 x 50gm
Crew neck	12	13	14	14	15	16 x 50gm

(mans laced neck sweater photographed in Rowanspun Aran in Husk 961, crew neck sweater in Rowanspun Aran in Atlantic 964)
★ Use Rowanspun DK **DOUBLE** throughout.

NEEDLES
1 pair 5mm (no 6) (US 8) needles
1 pair 5½mm (no 5) (US 9) needles

TENSION
16 sts and 23 rows to 10 cm measured over stocking stitch using 5½mm (US 9) needles and either **one strand** of Rowanspun Aran, or **two strands** of Rowanspun DK held together.

Pattern note: The pattern is written for the 5 childrens sizes, followed by the 3 ladies sizes in **bold**, followed by the 3 mens sizes. Where only one figure appears this applies to all sizes in that group.

Laced neck sweater
FRONT
Cast on 69 (75: 75: 81: 87: **89: 95: 95:** 101: 107: 107) sts using 5mm (US 8) needles.
Childrens sizes only
Row 1 (RS): K3, ★P3, K3, rep from ★ to end.
Row 2: P3, ★K3, P3, rep from ★ to end.
Ladies and mens sizes only
Row 1 (RS): K4, ★P3, K3, rep from ★ to last st, pick up loop lying between needles and place this loop on right needle (note: this loop does NOT count as a st), sl last st knitwise.
Row 2: P tog first st and the loop, P3, ★K3, P3, rep from ★ to last st, pick up loop lying between needles and place this loop on right needle (note: this loop does NOT count as a st), sl last st knitwise.
Row 3: K tog tbl first st and the loop, K3, ★P3, K3, rep from ★ to last st, pick up loop lying between needles and place this loop on right needle, sl last st knitwise.
Row 4: As row 2.
All sizes
Rep last 2 rows 5 (**6:** 7) times more, - (dec: inc: -: dec: **-: dec: inc:** -: dec: inc) 2 sts evenly across last row. 69 (73: 77: 81: 85: **89: 93: 97:** 101: 105: 109) sts.

Change to 5½mm (US 9) needles.
Beg with a K row, work in st st for 2 rows.
Starting and ending rows as indicated, work from chart for trellis patt as folls:
Work chart rows 1 to 8, and then rep chart row 1 again.
Beg with a **purl** row, cont in st st until front measures 21.5 (25.5: 28.5: 29: 33: **33: 34: 35:** 35: 32.5: 34) cm, ending with a WS row.
Starting and ending rows as indicated and repeating the 8 row repeat throughout, cont from chart for trellis patt as folls:
Cont straight until front measures 26 (29: 32: 35: 38: **41:** 41) cm, ending with a WS row.
Shape armholes
Cast off 4 sts at beg of next 2 rows.
61 (65: 69: 73: 77: **81: 85: 89:** 93: 97: 101) sts.
Dec 1 st at each end of next 1 (**4: 4**) rows, then on foll 1 (**0: 0**) alt row.
57 (61: 65: 69: 73: **73: 77: 81:** 85: 89: 93) sts.★★
Cont straight until armhole measures approx 4.5 (5: 5: 6: 7: **4.5: 5: 6:** 6: 7: 8.5) cm, ending after row 4 of trellis chart and with a WS row.
Starting and ending rows as indicated, working chart rows 1 to 10 once only and then repeating chart rows 11 to 18 throughout, cont from chart for yoke as folls:
Work 8 rows, ending with a WS row.
Divide for front opening
Next row (RS): Patt 22 (24: 26: 28: 30: **30: 32: 34:** 36: 38: 40) sts, yfwd, K2tog (for first eyelet), patt 4 sts and turn, leaving rem sts on a holder.
28 (30: 32: 34: 36: **36: 38: 40:** 42: 44: 46) sts.
Work each side of neck separately.
Working eyelets on every foll 8th row as set, cont from chart for yoke for a further 18 (**24: 24**) rows, ending after chart row 11 (**17: 17**) and a RS row. (3 (**4: 4**) eyelets made.)
Shape neck
Next row (WS): Patt 8 (**8: 9**) sts and slip these sts onto a holder, patt to end.
20 (22: 24: 26: 28: **28: 30: 32:** 33: 35: 37) sts.
Dec 1 st at neck edge on next 3 (3: 2: 2: 2: **3: 3**) rows, then on foll 2 (2: 3: 3: 3: **1: 1**) alt rows.
15 (17: 19: 21: 23: **24: 26: 28:** 29: 31: 33) sts.
Ladies and mens sizes only
Work 3 rows.
Dec 1 st at neck edge on next and foll 4th row.
- (**22: 24: 26:** 27: 29: 31) sts.
All sizes
Work 1 (1: 2: 2: 2: **3:** 3) rows, ending with a WS row. (Armhole should measure approx 20 (21: 22: 23: 24: **25: 26: 27:** 28: 29: 30) cm.)
Shape shoulder
Cast off 5 (6: 6: 7: 7: **7: 8: 9:** 9: 10: 10) sts at beg of next and foll alt row.
Work 1 row. Cast off rem 5 (5: 7: 7: 7: **8: 9: 9:** 11) sts.
With RS facing, rejoin yarn to rem sts and, beg with yoke chart row 9 cont as folls:
Next row (RS): K2tog, patt 3 sts, K2tog, yfwd (for first eyelet), patt to end.
28 (30: 32: 34: 36: **36: 38: 40:** 42: 44: 46) sts.
Complete to match first side, reversing shapings.

BACK
Work as given for front to ★★.
Working in trellis patt throughout, cont straight until back matches front to start of shoulder shaping, ending with a WS row.

Shape shoulders and back neck
Cast off 5 (6: 6: 7: 8: **7: 8: 9:** 9: 10: 10) sts at beg of next 2 rows.
47 (49: 53: 55: 57: **59: 61: 63:** 67: 69: 73) sts.
Next row (RS): Cast off 5 (6: 6: 7: 8: **7: 8: 9:** 9: 10: 10) sts, patt until there are 9 (9: 11: 11: 11: **12:** 13: 13: 15) sts on right needle and turn, leaving rem sts on a holder. Work each side of neck separately. Cast off 4 sts at beg of next row.
Cast off rem 5 (5: 7: 7: 7: **8:** 9: 9: 11) sts.
With RS facing, rejoin yarn to rem sts, cast off centre 19 (**21: 23**) sts, patt to end.
Work to match first side, reversing shapings.

SLEEVES (both alike)
Cast on 41 (41: 45: 45: 45: **49:** 53) sts using 5mm (US 8) needles.
Row 1 (RS): P1 (1: 0: 0: 0: **0:** 1), K3 (3: 0: 0: 0: **2:** 3), ★P3, K3, rep from ★ to last 1 (1: 3: 3: 3: **5:** 1) sts, P1 (1: 3: 3: 3: **3:** 1), K0 (**2:** 0).
Row 2: K1 (1: 0: 0: 0: **0:** 1), P3 (3: 0: 0: 0: **2:** 3), ★K3, P3, rep from ★ to last 1 (1: 3: 3: 3: **5:** 1) sts, K1 (1: 3: 3: 3: **3:** 1), P0 (**2:** 0).
These 2 rows form rib.
Work in rib for a further 10 (14: 16) rows, inc 1 st at each end of 5th (**9th:** 11th) of these rows.
43 (43: 47: 47: 47: **51:** 55) sts.
Change to 5½mm (US 9) needles. Beg with a K row, work in st st for 2 rows, inc 1 st at each end of first of these rows. 45 (45: 49: 49: 49: **53:** 57) sts.
Starting and ending rows as indicated, work from chart for trellis patt as folls:
Work chart rows 1 to 8, inc 1 st at each end of chart row 5, and then rep chart row 1 again.
47 (47: 51: 51: 51: **55:** 59) sts.

(Knitting instructions continued on page 84)

43 (45.5: 48: 50.5: 53: **55.5: 58: 60.5:** 63: 65.5: 68) cm
(17 (18: 19: 20: 21: **22: 23: 24:** 25: 26: 27) in)

Opposite: Hamish Sweater knitted in Rowanspun Chunky, knitting instructions on page 11

HAMISH

YARN

Rowan Rowanspun Chunky

To fit age	4-5	6-7	8-9	10-11	12-13	years
Polo neck	4	5	5	6	7	x 100gm
Shawl neck	4	4	5	6	6	x 100gm

(polo neck sweater photographed in Silver 984)

	ladies		mens			
	S	M	L	M	L	XL
To fit bust/chest	86	91	97	102	107	112	cm
	34	36	38	40	42	44	in
Polo neck	7	8	8	9	10	10	x100gm
Shawl neck	7	7	8	9	9	9	x100gm

(mans polo neck sweater photographed in Green Waters 982, shawl neck sweater in Blue Haze 985)

NEEDLES

1 pair 7mm (no 2) (US 10½) needles
1 pair 8mm (no 0) (US 11) needles

TENSION

12 sts and 16 rows to 10 cm measured over stocking stitch using 8mm (US 11) needles.

Pattern note: The pattern is written for the 5 childrens sizes, followed by the 3 ladies sizes in **bold**, followed by the 3 mens sizes. Where only one figure appears this applies to all sizes in that group.

Polo neck sweater

BACK

Cast on 46 (50: 54: 58: 62: **66: 70: 74:** 78: 82: 86) sts using 7mm (US 10½) needles.
Row 1 (RS): K0 (0: 2: 0: 0: **2: 0: 0:** 2: 0: 0), P0 (2: 2: 0: 2: **2: 0: 2:** 2: 0: 2), ★K4, P2, rep from ★ to last 4 (0: 2: 4: 0: **2: 4: 0:** 2: 4: 0) sts, K4 (0: 2: 4: 0: **2: 4: 0:** 2: 4: 0).
Row 2: P0 (0: 2: 0: 0: **2: 0: 0:** 2: 0: 0), K0 (2: 2: 0: 2: **2: 0: 2:** 2: 0: 2), ★P4, K2, rep from ★ to last 4 (0: 2: 4: 0: **2: 4: 0:** 2: 4: 0) sts, P4 (0: 2: 4: 0: **2: 4: 0:** 2: 4: 0).
Rep last 2 rows 3 (**4: 5**) times more.
Change to 8mm (US 11) needles.
Beg with a K row, work in st st until back measures 21 (25: 29: 33: 37: **41:** 41) cm, ending with a WS row.

Shape armholes

Cast off 5 (**2: 2**) sts at beg of next 2 rows.
36 (40: 44: 48: 52: **62: 66: 70:** 74: 78: 82) sts.

Ladies and mens sizes only
Next row (RS): K2, K3tog, K to last 5 sts, K3tog tbl, K2.
Next row: Purl.
Rep last 2 rows twice more.
– (**50: 54: 58:** 62: 66: 70) sts.

All sizes
Cont straight until armhole measures 19 (20: 21: 22: 23: **24: 25: 26:** 27: 28: 29) cm, ending with a WS row.

Shape shoulders and back neck

Cast off 3 (3: 4: 4: 5: **4: 5: 6:** 6: 7: 7) sts at beg of next 2 rows.
30 (34: 36: 40: 42: **42: 44: 46:** 50: 52: 56) sts.

Next row (RS): Cast off 3 (3: 4: 4: 5: **4: 5: 6:** 6: 7: 7) sts, K until there are 6 (8: 7: 9: 9: **9:** 10: 10: 12) sts on right needle and turn, leaving rem sts on a holder.
Work each side of neck separately.
Cast off 4 sts at beg of next row.
Cast off rem 2 (4: 3: 5: 5: **5:** 6: 6: 8) sts.
With RS facing, rejoin yarn to rem sts, cast off centre 12 (12: 14: 14: 14: **16:** 18) sts, K to end.
Work to match first side, reversing shapings.

FRONT

Work as given for back until 8 (**10:** 12) rows less have been worked to start of shoulder shaping, ending with a WS row.

Shape neck

Next row (RS): K12 (14: 15: 17: 19: **19: 21: 23:** 24: 26: 28) and turn, leaving rem sts on a holder.
Work each side of neck separately.

Childrens sizes only
Dec 1 st at neck edge on next 2 rows, then on foll 2 alt rows. 8 (10: 11: 13: 15: **–: –**) sts.

Ladies and mens sizes only
Work 1 row.
Working all decreases 2 sts in from neck edge in same way as for armhole decreases, dec 2 sts at neck edge of next and foll alt row, then on foll 4th row. – (**13: 15: 17:** 18: 20: 22) sts.

All sizes
Work 1 (**1:** 3) rows, ending with a WS row.

Shape shoulder

Cast off 3 (3: 4: 4: 5: **4: 5: 6:** 6: 7: 7) sts at beg of next and foll alt row.
Work 1 row. Cast off rem 2 (4: 3: 5: 5: **5:** 6: 6: 8) sts.
With RS facing, rejoin yarn to rem sts, cast off centre 12 (12: 14: 14: 14: **12:** 14) sts, K to end.
Work to match first side, reversing shapings.

SLEEVES (both alike)

Cast on 26 (28: 30: 32: 34: **36: 36: 38:** 40: 40: 42) sts using 7mm (US 10½) needles.
Row 1 (RS): P0 (1: 1: 0: 0), K0 (1: 2: 3: 4: **4: 4: 0:** 1: 1: 2), ★P2, K4, rep from ★ to last 2 (3: 4: 5: 6: **1: 1: 2:** 3: 3: 4) sts, P2 (1: 1: 2: 2), K0 (1: 2: 3: 4: **0:** 1: 1: 2).
Row 2: K0 (1: 1: 0: 0), P0 (1: 2: 3: 4: **4: 4: 0:** 1: 1: 2), ★K2, P4, rep from ★ to last 2 (3: 4: 5: 6: **1: 1: 2:** 3: 3: 4) sts, K2 (1: 1: 2: 2), P0 (1: 2: 3: 4: **0:** 1: 1: 2).
Rep last 2 rows 3 (**4: 5**) times more.
Change to 8mm (US 11) needles.
Beg with a K row, cont in st st, shaping sides by inc 1 st at each end of next and every foll 4th (4th: 6th: 6th: 6th: **6th:** 6th) row to 36 (44: 34: 42: 48: **48: 46: 52:** 54: 48: 52) sts, then on every foll alt (alt: 4th: 4th: 4th: **4th:** 4th) row until there are 46 (48: 50: 52: 56: **58: 60: 62:** 64: 68: 70) sts.
Cont straight until sleeve measures 28 (32: 36: 40: 44: **42: 44: 46:** 48: 49: 50) cm from cast-on edge, ending with a WS row.

Childrens sizes only
Cast off.

Ladies and mens sizes only
Shape top
Cast off – (**2:** 2) sts at beg of next 2 rows.
– (**54: 56: 58:** 60: 64: 66) sts.
Work 2 rows.
Working all decreases 2 sts in from ends of rows in same way as for armhole decreases, dec 2 sts at each end of next and foll 4th row.

Work 3 rows, ending with a WS row.
Cast off rem – (**46: 48: 50:** 52: 56: 58) sts.

Shawl neck sweater
BACK
Work as given for back of polo neck sweater.
FRONT
Work as given for back until 16 (**18:** 20) rows less have been worked to start of shoulder shaping, ending with a WS row.
Shape neck
Next row (RS): K8 (10: 11: 13: 15: **13: 15: 17:** 18: 20: 22) and turn, leaving rem sts on a holder.
Work each side of neck separately.
Work 15 (**17:** 19) rows, ending with a WS row.
Shape shoulder
Cast off 3 (3: 4: 4: 5: **4: 5: 6:** 6: 7: 7) sts at beg of next and foll alt row.
Work 1 row.
Cast off rem 2 (4: 3: 5: 5: **5:** 6: 6: 8) sts.
With RS facing, rejoin yarn to rem sts, cast off centre 20 (20: 22: 22: 22: **24:** 26) sts, K to end.
Work to match first side, reversing shapings.

SLEEVES (both alike)
Work as given for sleeves of polo neck sweater.

MAKING UP
PRESS all pieces as described on the info page.
Polo neck sweater
Join right shoulder seam using back stitch, or mattress stitch if preferred.
Collar
With RS facing and 7mm (US 10½) needles, pick up and knit 12 (**15:** 16) sts down left side of neck, 11 (11: 14: 14: 14: **12:** 14) sts from front, 12 (**15:** 16) sts up right side of neck, then 19 (19: 22: 22: 22: **24:** 26) sts from back. 54 (54: 60: 60: 60: **66:** 72) sts.

(Size diagrams and knitting instructions continued on page 83)

Opposite: Hamish Polo & Shawl Necks both knitted in Rowanspun Chunky

EILEAN

YARN

Rowan Rowanspun Aran

	XS	S	M	L	XL	
To fit bust	81	86	91	97	102	cm
	32	34	36	38	40	in
A Igloo	960	7	8	8	8	9 x 100gm
B Husk	961	2	2	2	3	3 x 100gm

NEEDLES

1 pair 4½mm (no 7) (US 7) needles
1 pair 5½mm (no 5) (US 9) needles

TENSION

16 sts and 23 rows to 10 cm measured over patterned stocking stitch using 5½mm (US 9) needles.

BACK

Cast on 90 (94: 98: 102: 106) sts using 4½mm (US 7) needles and yarn A.
Row 1 (RS): *K1, P1, rep from * to end.
Row 2: *P1, K1, rep from * to end.
These 2 rows form moss st.
Work in moss st for a further 2 rows, ending with a WS row.
Using a combination of the **fairisle** technique (for rows 1 to 4 and rows 25 to 28) and the **intarsia** technique (for all other rows) as described on the information page, starting and ending rows as indicated, cont in patt foll chart as folls:
Work chart rows 1 to 8.
Change to 5½mm (US 9) needles. Repeating the 24 row repeat throughout and now working entirely in st st, cont straight until back measures 45 (46: 46: 47: 47) cm, ending with a WS row.
Shape armholes
Keeping patt correct, cast off 4 sts at beg of next 2 rows. 82 (86: 90: 94: 98) sts.
Dec 1 st at each end of next 6 rows.
70 (74: 78: 82: 86) sts.
Cont straight until armhole measures 25 (25: 26: 26: 27) cm, ending with a WS row.
Shape shoulders and back neck
Keeping patt correct, cast off 5 (6: 6: 7: 7) sts at beg of next 2 rows. 60 (62: 66: 68: 72) sts.
Next row (RS): Cast off 5 (6: 6: 7: 7) sts, patt until there are 10 (9: 11: 10: 12) sts on right needle and turn, leaving rem sts on a holder.
Work each side of neck separately.
Cast off 4 sts at beg of next row.

Cast off rem 6 (5: 7: 6: 8) sts.
With RS facing, rejoin yarn to rem sts, cast off centre 30 (32: 32: 34: 34) sts, patt to end.
Work to match first side, reversing shapings.

FRONT

Work as given for back until 2 rows less have been worked to start of shoulder shaping, ending with a WS row.
Shape neck
Next row (RS): Patt 20 (21: 23: 24: 26) sts and turn, leaving rem sts on a holder.
Work each side of neck separately.
Dec 1 st at neck edge on next row.
19 (20: 22: 23: 25) sts.
Shape shoulder
Keeping patt correct, cast off 5 (6: 6: 7: 7) sts at beg and dec 1 st at end of next row.
13 (13: 15: 15: 17) sts.
Dec 1 st at neck edge of next row.
12 (12: 14: 14: 16) sts.
Cast off 5 (6: 6: 7: 7) sts at beg and dec 1 st at end of next row. 6 (5: 7: 6: 8) sts.
Work 1 row. Cast off rem 6 (5: 7: 6: 8) sts.
With RS facing, rejoin yarn to rem sts, cast off centre 30 (32: 32: 34: 34) sts, patt to end.
Work to match first side, reversing shapings.

SLEEVES (both alike)

Cast on 56 (56: 58: 60: 60) sts using 4½mm (US 7) needles and yarn A.
Row 1 (RS): K1 (1: 0: 1: 1), *P1, K1, rep from * to last 1 [1: 0: 1: 1] st, P1 [1: 0: 1: 1].
Row 2: P1 (1: 0: 1: 1), *K1, P1, rep from * to last 1 [1: 0: 1: 1] st, K1 [1: 0: 1: 1].
Rep last 2 rows once more, ending with a WS row.
Using a combination of the **fairisle** technique (for rows 1 to 4 and rows 25 to 28) and the **intarsia** technique (for all other rows) as described on the information page, starting and ending rows as indicated, cont in patt foll chart as folls:
Work chart rows 1 to 8.
Change to 5½mm (US 9) needles.
Repeating the 24 row repeat throughout and now working entirely in st st, cont in patt foll chart as folls:
Inc 1 st at each end of 3rd and every foll 8th row to 74 (74: 72: 80: 68) sts, then on every foll 6th row until there are 80 (80: 84: 84: 88) sts, taking inc sts into patt.

Cont straight until sleeve measures 44 (44: 45: 45: 45) cm, ending with a WS row.
Shape top
Cast off 4 sts at beg of next 2 rows.
72 (72: 76: 76: 80) sts.
Dec 1 st at each end of next and foll 5 alt rows.
Work 1 row, ending with a WS row.
Cast off rem 60 (60: 64: 64: 68) sts.

MAKING UP

PRESS all pieces as described on the info page.
Join right shoulder seam using back stitch, or mattress stitch if preferred.
Neckband
With RS facing, 4½mm (US 7) needles and yarn A, pick up and knit 6 sts down left side of neck, 30 (32: 32: 34: 34) sts from front, 6 sts up right side of neck, then 38 (40: 40: 42: 42) sts from back.
80 (84: 84: 88: 88) sts.
Row 1 (WS): *K1, P1, rep from * to end.
Row 2: *P1, K1, rep from * to end.
These 2 rows form moss st.
Work in moss st for a further 3 rows.
Join in yarn B.
Row 6 (RS): *Using yarn B K1, using yarn A K3, rep from * to end.
Row 7: Using yarn B P2, *using yarn A P1, using yarn B P3, rep from * to last 2 sts, using yarn A P1, using yarn B P1.
Row 8: Using yarn B K2, *using yarn A K1, using yarn B K3, rep from * to last 2 sts, using yarn A K1, using yarn B K1.
Row 9: *Using yarn B P1, using yarn A P3, rep from * to end.
Break off yarn B and cont using yarn A only.
Beg next row with a P st, work in moss st for 5 rows.
Cast off in moss st.
See information page for finishing instructions, setting in sleeves using the shallow set-in method.

Opposite, from left to right: Eilean Sweater knitted in Rowanspun Aran, Calum Jacket knitted in Rowanspun Aran knitting instructions on page 59, & Heather Sweater knitted in Kid Classic, knitting instructions on page 14

Key □ Using yarn A, K on RS, P on WS ▨ Using yarn A, P on RS, K on WS ■ Using yarn B, K on RS, P on WS

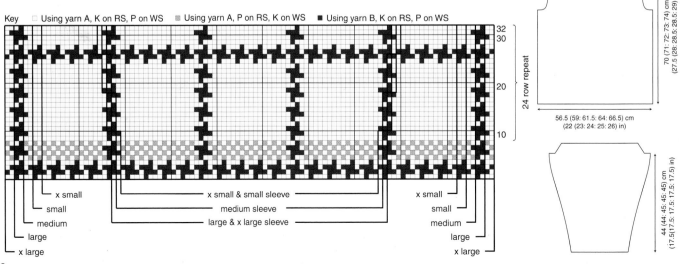

HEATHER

YARN
Rowan Kid Classic

	XS	S	M	L	XL	
To fit bust	81	86	91	97	102cm	
	32	34	36	38	40 in	
Sweater	7	8	8	8	9 x	50gm
Cardigan	8	8	8	9	9 x	50gm

(sweater photographed in Thyme 826, cardigan in Swirl 834)

NEEDLES
1 pair 4½mm (no 7) (US 7) needles
1 pair 5mm (no 6) (US 8) needles
Cable needle

STUD FASTENERS - 6 for cardigan

TENSION
19 sts and 25 rows to 10 cm measured over stocking stitch using 5mm (US 8) needles.

SPECIAL ABBREVIATIONS
C10F = Cable 10 front Slip next 5 sts onto cable needle and leave at front of work, K5, then K5 from cable needle.

C10B = Cable 10 back Slip next 5 sts onto cable needle and leave at back of work, K5, then K5 from cable needle.

Sweater
BACK
Cast on 108 (112: 118: 122: 128) sts using 4½mm (US 7) needles.
Row 1 (RS): P0 (0: 2: 0: 0), K7 (9: 10: 1: 4), *P3, K10, rep from * to last 10 (12: 2: 4: 7) sts, P3 (3: 2: 3: 3), K7 (9: 0: 1: 4).
Row 2: K0 (0: 2: 0: 0), P7 (9: 10: 1: 4), *K3, P10, rep from * to last 10 (12: 2: 4: 7) sts, K3 (3: 2: 3: 3), P7 (9: 0: 1: 4).
These 2 rows form rib.
Work in rib for a further 8 rows, ending with a WS row.
Change to 5mm (US 8) needles.
Cont in rib, dec 1 st at each end of 5th and every foll 6th row until 102 (106: 112: 116: 122) sts rem.
Work 3 rows, ending with a WS row.
Place cables
Next row (RS): Rib 7 (9: 12: 14: 17), C10B, rib 16, C10B, rib 16, C10F, rib 16, C10F, rib 7 (9: 12: 14: 17).
Keeping rib correct and working cables as set by last row on every foll 20th row, cont as folls:
Work 1 row, ending with a WS row.
Dec 1 st at each end of next and foll 6th row. 98 (102: 108: 112: 118) sts.
Work 9 rows, ending with a WS row.
Inc 1 st at each end of next and every foll 8th row to 106 (110: 116: 120: 126) sts, then on foll 6th row, taking inc sts into rib. 108 (112: 118: 122: 128) sts.
Cont straight until back measures 34 (35: 35: 36: 36) cm, ending with a WS row.
Shape armholes
Keeping patt correct, cast off 3 (4: 4: 5: 5) sts at beg of next 2 rows. 102 (104: 110: 112: 118) sts.
Dec 1 st at each end of next 3 (3: 5: 5: 7) rows, then on foll 2 alt rows. 92 (94: 96: 98: 100) sts.
Cont straight until armhole measures 22 (22: 23: 23: 24) cm, ending with a WS row.

Shape shoulders and back neck
Keeping patt correct, cast off 9 (9: 9: 10: 10) sts at beg of next 2 rows. 74 (76: 78: 78: 80) sts.
Next row (RS): Cast off 9 (9: 9: 10: 10) sts, patt until there are 12 (13: 14: 13: 14) sts on right needle and turn, leaving rem sts on a holder.
Work each side of neck separately.
Cast off 4 sts at beg of next row.
Cast off rem 8 (9: 10: 9: 10) sts.
With RS facing, rejoin yarn to rem sts, cast off centre 32 sts, patt to end.
Work to match first side, reversing shapings.

FRONT
Work as given for back until 18 rows less have been worked to start of shoulder shaping, ending with a WS row.
Shape neck
Next row (RS): Patt 35 (36: 37: 38: 39) sts and turn, leaving rem sts on a holder.
Work each side of neck separately.
Cast off 4 sts at beg of next row.
31 (32: 33: 34: 35) sts.
Dec 1 st at neck edge on next 3 rows, then on foll alt row, then on foll 4th row.
26 (27: 28: 29: 30) sts.
Work 7 rows, ending with a WS row.
Shape shoulder
Keeping patt correct, cast off 9 (9: 9: 10: 10) sts at beg of next and foll alt row.
Work 1 row.
Cast off rem 8 (9: 10: 9: 10) sts.
With RS facing, slip centre 22 sts onto a holder, rejoin yarn to rem sts, patt to end.
Work to match first side, reversing shapings.

LEFT SLEEVE
Cast on 48 (48: 50: 52: 52) sts using 4½mm (US 7) needles.
Row 1 (RS): P3 (3: 4: 5: 5), (K5, P3) twice, K10, (P3, K5) twice, P3 (3: 4: 5: 5).
Row 2: K3 (3: 4: 5: 5), (P5, K3) twice, P10, (K3, P5) twice, K3 (3: 4: 5: 5).
Rep last 2 rows 9 times more, ending with a WS row.
Change to 5mm (US 8) needles.
Row 1 (RS): Inc in first st, K15 (15: 16: 17: 17), P3, K10, P3, K15 (15: 16: 17: 17), inc in last st.
50 (50: 52: 54: 54) sts.
Row 2: P17 (17: 18: 19: 19), K3, P10, K3, P17 (17: 18: 19: 19).
These 2 rows set the sts.
Work a further 8 rows, inc 1 st at each end of 0 (0: 0: 0: 7th) of these rows and ending with a WS row. 50 (50: 52: 54: 56) sts.
Place cable
Next row (RS): (Inc in first st) 1 (1: 1: 1: 0) time, K16 (16: 17: 18: 20), P3, C10F, P3, K16 (16: 17: 18: 20), (inc in last st) 1 (1: 1: 1: 0) time.
52 (52: 54: 56: 56) sts.
Keeping sts correct and working cable as set by last row on every foll 20th row, cont as folls:
Inc 1 st at each end of 10th (10th: 10th: 10th: 8th) and every foll 10th (-: 10th: 10th: 8th) row to 62 (54: 58: 60: 72) sts, then on every foll 8th (8th: 8th: 8th: 6th) row until there are 66 (68: 70: 72: 74) sts, taking inc sts into st st.
Cont straight until sleeve measures 43 (43: 44: 44: 44) cm, ending with a WS row.

Shape top
Keeping patt correct, cast off 3 (4: 4: 5: 5) sts at beg of next 2 rows. 60 (60: 62: 62: 64) sts.
Dec 1 st at each end of next 3 rows, then on foll 2 alt rows, then on every foll 4th row until 40 (40: 42: 42: 44) sts rem.
Work 1 row, ending with a WS row.
Dec 1 st at each end of next and foll 1 (1: 2: 2: 3) alt rows, then on foll 3 rows.
Cast off rem 30 sts.

RIGHT SLEEVE
Work as given for left sleeve but working cable as "C10B" in place of "C10F".

Cardigan
BACK
Work as given for back of sweater.

LEFT FRONT
Note: The front bands are knitted at the same time as the fronts. The front opening edge 10 sts will be folded to the WS and the finished front edge is marked by the slipped stitch.
Cast on 70 (72: 75: 77: 80) sts using 4½mm (US 7) needles.
Row 1 (RS): P0 (0: 2: 0: 0), K7 (9: 10: 1: 4), *P3, K10, rep from * to last 24 sts, P3, K10, slip next st purlwise, K10.
Row 2: P21, *K3, P10, rep from * to last 10 (12: 2: 4: 7) sts, K3 (3: 2: 3: 3), P7 (9: 0: 1: 4).
These 2 rows set the sts.
Cont as set for a further 8 rows, end with a WS row.
Change to 5mm (US 8) needles.
Cont as set, dec 1 st at beg of 5th and every foll 6th row until 67 (69: 72: 74: 77) sts rem.
Work 3 rows, ending with a WS row.
Place cables
Next row (RS): Rib 7 (9: 12: 14: 17), C10B, rib 16, C10B, patt 24 sts.
Keeping sts correct and working cables as set by last row on every foll 20th row, cont as folls:
Work 1 row, ending with a WS row.
Dec 1 st at beg of next and foll 6th row.
65 (67: 70: 72: 75) sts.
Work 9 rows, ending with a WS row.
Inc 1 st at beg of next and every foll 8th row to 69 (71: 74: 76: 79) sts, then on foll 6th row, taking inc sts into rib. 70 (72: 75: 77: 80) sts.
Cont straight until left front matches back to beg of armhole shaping, ending with a WS row.
Shape armhole
Keeping patt correct, cast off 3 (4: 4: 5: 5) sts at beg of next row. 67 (68: 71: 72: 75) sts.
Work 1 row.
Dec 1 st at armhole edge of next 3 (3: 5: 5: 7) rows, then on foll 2 alt rows. 62 (63: 64: 65: 66) sts.
Cont straight until 19 rows less have been worked than on back to start of shoulder shaping, ending with a RS row.
Shape neck
Next row (RS): Patt 27 sts and slip these sts onto a holder, patt to end. 35 (36: 37: 38: 39) sts.
Work 1 row.
Cast off 4 sts at beg of next row. 31 (32: 33: 34: 35) sts.
Dec 1 st at neck edge on next 3 rows, then on foll alt row then on foll 4th row.
26 (27: 28: 29: 30) sts.
Work 7 rows, ending with a WS row.

Shape shoulder

Keeping patt correct, cast off 9 (9: 9: 10: 10) sts at beg of next and foll alt row.
Work 1 row.
Cast off rem 8 (9: 10: 9: 10) sts.

RIGHT FRONT

Cast on 70 (72: 75: 77: 80) sts using 4¹/₂mm (US 7) needles.
Row 1 (RS): K10, slip next st purlwise, K10, P3, ★K10, P3, rep from ★ to last 7 (9: 12: 1: 4) sts, K7 (9: 10: 1: 4), P0 (0: 2: 0: 0).
Row 2: P7 (9: 0: 1: 4), K3 (3: 2: 3: 3), ★P10, K3, rep from ★ to last 21 sts, P21.
These 2 rows set the sts.
Cont as set for a further 8 rows, end with a WS row.
Change to 5mm (US 8) needles.
Cont as set, dec 1 st at end of 5th and every foll 6th row until 67 (69: 72: 74: 77) sts rem.
Work 3 rows, ending with a WS row.

Place cables

Next row (RS): Patt 24 sts, C10F, rib 16, C10F, rib 7 (9: 12: 14: 17).
Keeping sts correct and working cables as set by last row on every foll 20th row, complete to match left front, reversing shapings.

SLEEVES

Work as given for sleeves of sweater.

MAKING UP

PRESS all pieces as described on the info page.
Sweater
Join right shoulder seam using back stitch, or mattress stitch if preferred.
Neckband
With RS facing and 4¹/₂mm (US 7) needles, pick up and knit 21 sts down left side of neck, patt across 22 sts from front holder, pick up and knit 21 sts up right side of neck, then 32 sts from back. 96 sts.

Row 1 (WS): (K3, P5) 7 times, K3, P10, K3, (P5, K3) 3 times.
Row 2: (P3, K5) 3 times, P3, K10, P3, (K5, P3) 7 times.
Rep last 2 rows for 10 cm.
Cast off in rib.
See information page for finishing instructions, setting in sleeves using the set-in method.
Cardigan
Join shoulder seams using back stitch, or mattress stitch if preferred.
Neckband
With RS facing and 4¹/₂mm (US 7) needles, slip 27 sts from right front holder onto right needle, pick up and knit 19 sts up right side of neck, 41 sts from back, and 19 sts down left side of neck, then patt across 27 sts from left front holder. 133 sts.
Row 1 (WS): P21, K3, ★P5, K3, rep from ★ to last 21 sts, P21.
Row 2: K10, slip next st purlwise, K10, P3, ★K5, P3, rep from ★ to last 21 sts, K10, slip next st purlwise, K10.
Rep last 2 rows until neckband measures 3 cm.
Cast off in rib.
Fold front opening edges to inside along line of slipped sts and sew in place. Attach top half of stud fasteners to right front facing (on inside), spacing them centrally across and evenly along facing. Attach other half of stud fasteners to outside of left front to correspond, so that front borders overlap.
See information page for finishing instructions, setting in sleeves using the set-in method.

56 (57: 58: 59: 60) cm
(22 (22.5: 23: 23: 23.5) in)

46.5 (48.5: 51.5: 53.5: 57) cm
(18.5 (19: 20.5: 21: 22.5) in)

43 (43: 44: 44: 44) cm
(17 (17: 17.5: 17.5: 17.5) in)

From left to right: Eilean Sweater knitted in Rowanspun Aran, knitting instructions on page 12, Calum Jacket knitted in Rowanspun Aran knitting instructions on page 59, & Heather Sweater knitted in Kid Classic

From left to right: Nevis Cardigan, knitting instructions on page 69, Firth Jacket, knitting instructions on page 33, Hamish Sweater, knitting instructions on page 11, Thistle Jacket, knitting instructions on page 65 & Spencer Sweater, knitting instructions on page 49

BONNY

YARN
Rowan Felted Tweed or Kidsilk Haze

	XS	S	M	L	XL
To fit bust	81	86	91	97	102 cm
	32	34	36	38	40 in

Rowan Felted Tweed

	7	7	7	8	8 x	50gm

(photographed in Treacle 145)

Rowan Kidsilk Haze★

A Pearl	590	5	5	5	6	6 x	25gm
B Chill	591	5	5	5	6	6 x	25gm

★Use Kidsilk Haze **DOUBLE** throughout, using one strand of yarn A held together with one strand of yarn B.

For one colour sweater in Kidsilk Haze (not photographed), you will need 9 (9: 10: 11: 11) x 25 gm balls of same colour.

NEEDLES
1 pair 3¼mm (no 10) (US 3) needles
1 pair 3¾mm (no 9) (US 5) needles

TENSION
23 sts and 32 rows to 10 cm measured over stocking stitch using 3¾mm (US 5) needles and either **one strand** of Felted Tweed, or **two strands** of Kidsilk Haze held together.

BACK and FRONT (both alike)
Cast on 103 (109: 115: 121: 127) sts using 3¼mm (US 3) needles.
Knit 3 rows, ending with a RS row.
Now work in moss st as folls:
Row 1 (WS): K1, *P1, K1, rep from * to end.
Row 2: As row 1.
These 2 rows form moss st.
Work in moss st for a further 17 rows, ending with a WS row.
Change to 3¾mm (US 5) needles.
Beg with a K row, work in st st, shaping sides by inc 1 st at each end of next and every foll 18th row until there are 111 (117: 123: 129: 135) sts.
Cont straight until work measures 28 cm, ending with a WS row.
Shape raglan armholes
Cast off 4 sts at beg of next 2 rows.
103 (109: 115: 121: 127) sts.
Extra small size only
Next row (RS): P2, K1, K2tog, yfwd, K2tog, K to last 7 sts, K2tog tbl, yfwd, K2tog tbl, K1, P2.
101 sts.
Next row: K2, P to last 2 sts, K2.
Next row: P2, K1, K2tog, yfwd, K to last 5 sts, yfwd, K2tog tbl, K1, P2.
Next row: K2, P to last 2 sts, K2.
Medium, large and extra large sizes only
Next row (RS): P2, K1, K2tog, yfwd, K3tog, K to last 8 sts, K3tog tbl, yfwd, K2tog tbl, K1, P2.
Next row: K2, P to last 2 sts, K2.
Rep last 2 rows – (–: 1: 2: 4) times more.
– (–: 107: 109: 107) sts.
All sizes
Next row (RS): P2, K1, K2tog, yfwd, K2tog, K to last 7 sts, K2tog tbl, yfwd, K2tog tbl, K1, P2.
Next row: K2, P to last 2 sts, K2.
Rep last 2 rows 31 (34: 33: 33: 32) times more.
Break yarn and leave rem 37 (39: 39: 41: 41) sts on a holder.

SLEEVES (both alike)
Cast on 59 (59: 61: 63: 63) sts using 3¼mm (US 3) needles.
Knit 3 rows, ending with a RS row.
Work in moss st as given for back for 19 rows, shaping sides by inc 1 st at each end of 8th (8th: 8th: 8th: 6th) and foll 10th (8th: 10th: 10th: 8th) row. 63 (63: 65: 67: 67) sts.
Change to 3¾mm (US 5) needles.
Beg with a K row, work in st st, shaping sides by inc 1 st at each end of 9th (5th: 7th: 7th: 3rd) and every foll 10th (8th: 8th: 8th: 8th) row to 69 (93: 95: 97: 95) sts, then on every foll 8th (–: –: –: 6th) row until there are 91 (–: –: –: 99) sts.
Cont straight until sleeve measures 48 (48: 49: 49: 49) cm, ending with a WS row.
Shape raglan
Cast off 4 sts at beg of next 2 rows.
83 (85: 87: 89: 91) sts.
Next row (RS): P2, K1, K2tog, yfwd, K2tog, K to last 7 sts, K2tog tbl, yfwd, K2tog tbl, K1, P2.
Next row: K2, P to last 2 sts, K2.
Next row: P2, K1, K2tog, yfwd, K to last 5 sts, yfwd, K2tog tbl, K1, P2.
Next row: K2, P to last 2 sts, K2.
Rep last 4 rows once more. 79 (81: 83: 85: 87) sts.
Next row (RS): P2, K1, K2tog, yfwd, K2tog, K to last 7 sts, K2tog tbl, yfwd, K2tog tbl, K1, P2.
Next row: K2, P to last 2 sts, K2.
Rep last 2 rows 29 (30: 31: 32: 33) times more.
Break yarn and leave rem 19 sts on a holder.

MAKING UP
PRESS all pieces as described on the info page.
Join both front and right back raglan seams using back stitch, or mattress stitch if preferred.
Plain neckband
With RS facing and 3¼mm (US 3) needles, K first 18 sts of left sleeve, K tog last st of left sleeve with first st of front, K next 35 (37: 37: 39: 39) sts of front, K tog last st of front with first st of right sleeve, K next 17 sts of right sleeve, K tog last st of right sleeve with first st of back, K rem 36 (38: 38: 40: 40) sts of back.
109 (113: 113: 117: 117) sts.
Beg with a P row, work in st st for 7 rows.
Cast off **loosely** knitways.
Patterned neckband
With RS facing and 3¼mm (US 3) needles, work across first 18 sts of left sleeve as folls: P2, K1, K2tog, yfwd, K2tog, (P1, K1) twice, P1, K2tog tbl, yfwd, K2tog tbl, K1, P1, P tog last st of left sleeve with first st of front, work across next 35 (37: 37: 39: 39) sts of front as folls: P1, K1, K2tog, yfwd, K2tog, (P1, K1) 11 (12: 12: 13: 13) times, P1, K2tog tbl, yfwd, K2tog tbl, K1, P1, P tog last st of front with first st of right sleeve, work across next 17 sts of right sleeve as folls: P1, K1, K2tog, yfwd, K2tog, (P1, K1) twice, P1, K2tog tbl, yfwd, K2tog tbl, K1, P1, P tog last st of right sleeve with first st of back, work across rem 36 (38: 38: 40: 40) sts of back as folls: P1, K1, K2tog, yfwd, K2tog, (P1, K1) 11 (12: 12: 13: 13) times, P1, K2tog tbl, yfwd, K2tog tbl, K1, P2.
101 (105: 105: 109: 109) sts.
Keeping moss st correct as now set, cont as folls:
Row 1 (WS): K2, P3, moss st 7 sts, P3, K3, P3, moss st 25 (27: 27: 29: 29) sts, P3, K3, P3, moss st 7 sts, P3, K3, P3, moss st 25 (27: 27: 29: 29) sts, P3, K2.

Row 2: P2, K1, K2tog, yfwd, work 2 tog, moss st 3 sts, work 2 tog, yfwd, K2tog tbl, K1, P3, K1, K2tog, yfwd, work 2 tog, moss st 21 (23: 23: 25: 25) sts, work 2 tog, yfwd, K2tog tbl, K1, P3, K1, K2tog, yfwd, work 2 tog, moss st 3 sts, work 2 tog, yfwd, K2tog tbl, K1, P3, K1, K2tog, yfwd, work 2 tog, moss st 21 (23: 23: 25: 25) sts, work 2 tog, yfwd, K2tog tbl, K1, P2. 93 (97: 97: 101: 101) sts.
Row 3: K2, P3, moss st 5 sts, P3, K3, P3, moss st 23 (25: 25: 27: 27) sts, P3, K3, P3, moss st 5 sts, P3, K3, P3, moss st 23 (25: 25: 27: 27) sts, P3, K2.
Row 4: P2, K1, K2tog, yfwd, work 2 tog, moss st 1 st, work 2 tog, yfwd, K2tog tbl, K1, P3, K1, K2tog, yfwd, work 2 tog, moss st 19 (21: 21: 23: 23) sts, work 2 tog, yfwd, K2tog tbl, K1, P3, K1, K2tog, yfwd, work 2 tog, moss st 1 st, work 2 tog, yfwd, K2tog tbl, K1, P3, K1, K2tog, yfwd, work 2 tog, moss st 19 (21: 21: 23: 23) sts, work 2 tog, yfwd, K2tog tbl, K1, P2. 85 (89: 89: 93: 93) sts.
Row 5: K2, P3, moss st 3 sts, P3, K3, P3, moss st 21 (23: 23: 25: 25) sts, P3, K3, P3, moss st 3 sts, P3, K3, P3, moss st 21 (23: 23: 25: 25) sts, P3, K2.
Cast off in patt.
See information page for finishing instructions.

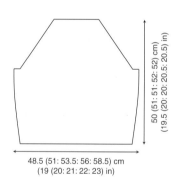

48.5 (51: 53.5: 56: 58.5) cm
(19 (20: 21: 22: 23) in)

50 (51: 51: 52: 52) cm
(19.5 (20: 20: 20.5: 20.5) in)

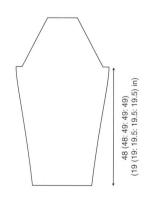

48 (48: 49: 49: 49)
(19 (19: 19.5: 19.5: 19.5) in)

Opposite: Bonny Sweater knitted in Kidsilk Haze, Bay Beret knitted in Lurex Shimmer, knitting instructions on page 77 & Firth Jacket knitted in Kid Classic knitting instructions on page 33

OAKLEY

YARN
Rowan Rowanspun 4 ply

		XS	S	M	L	XL	
To fit bust		81	86	91	97	102	cm
		32	34	36	38	40	in
A Swarm	701	8	8	8	9	9	x 25gm
B Rumtoft	703	2	2	2	2	2	x 25gm
C Sludge	711	2	2	2	2	2	x 25gm
D Sp. Orange	705	1	1	1	1	1	x 25gm

NEEDLES
1 pair 2¼mm (no 13) (US 1) needles
1 pair 3mm (no 11) (US 2/3) needles

BUTTONS - 7

TENSION
28 sts and 40 rows to 10 cm measured over patterned stocking stitch using 3mm (US 2/3) needles.

BACK
Cast on 135 (143: 151: 159: 167) sts using 2¼mm (US 1) needles and yarn A.
Row 1 (RS): K1, *P1, K1, rep from * to end.
Row 2: As row 1.
These 2 rows form moss st. Work in moss st for a further 10 rows, ending with a WS row.
Join in yarn B.
Row 13 (RS): Using yarn A K1, *using yarn B K1, using yarn A K1, rep from * to end.
Break off yarn B.
Work in moss st for a further 12 rows, ending with a RS row. Purl 1 row.
Change to 3mm (US 2/3) needles.
Using the **intarsia** technique as described on the information page and starting and ending rows as indicated, cont in patt foll chart for back (see page 22), which is worked entirely in st st, as folls:
Cont straight until chart row 106 (110: 110: 114: 114) has been completed, ending with a WS row.
Shape armholes
Keeping chart correct, cast off 5 (6: 6: 7: 7) sts at beg of next 2 rows. 125 (131: 139: 145: 153) sts.
Dec 1 st at each end of next 7 (7: 9: 9: 11) rows, then on foll 6 (7: 7: 8: 8) alt rows.
99 (103: 107: 111: 115) sts.
Cont straight until chart row 186 (190: 194: 198: 202) has been completed, ending with a WS row.
Shape shoulders and back neck
Keeping chart correct, cast off 9 (10: 10: 11: 11) sts at beg of next 2 rows. 81 (83: 87: 89: 93) sts.
Next row (RS): Cast off 9 (10: 10: 11: 11) sts, patt until there are 14 (13: 15: 14: 16) sts on right needle and turn, leaving rem sts on a holder.
Work each side of neck separately.
Cast off 4 sts at beg of next row.
Cast off rem 10 (9: 11: 10: 12) sts.
With RS facing, rejoin yarn to rem sts, cast off centre 35 (37: 37: 39: 39) sts, patt to end.
Work to match first side, reversing shapings.

LEFT FRONT
Cast on 76 (80: 84: 88: 92) sts using 2¼mm (US 1) needles and yarn A.
Row 1 (RS): *K1, P1, rep from * to end.
Row 2: *P1, K1, rep from * to end.
These 2 rows form moss st.
Work in moss st for a further 10 rows, ending with a WS row.

Join in yarn B.
Row 13 (RS): *Using yarn A K1, using yarn B K1, rep from * to last 6 sts, using yarn A (K1, P1) 3 times.
Break off yarn B.
Work in moss st for a further 12 rows, ending with a RS row.
Next row (WS): Moss st 16 sts and slip these sts onto a holder, P to end. 60 (64: 68: 72: 76) sts.
Change to 3mm (US 2/3) needles.
Starting and ending rows as indicated and omitting any incomplete motifs, cont in patt foll chart for fronts as folls:
Cont straight until chart row 106 (110: 110: 114: 114) has been completed, ending with a WS row.
Shape armhole
Keeping chart correct, cast off 5 (6: 6: 7: 7) sts at beg of next row. 55 (58: 62: 65: 69) sts.
Work 1 row.
Dec 1 st at armhole edge of next 7 (7: 9: 9: 11) rows, then on foll 6 (7: 7: 8: 8) alt rows.
42 (44: 46: 48: 50) sts.
Cont straight until chart row 159 (163: 167: 169: 173) has been completed, ending with a RS row.
Shape neck
Keeping chart correct, cast off 5 (6: 6: 6: 6) sts at beg of next row. 37 (38: 40: 42: 44) sts.
Dec 1 st at neck edge of next 3 rows, then on foll 4 (4: 4: 5: 5) alt rows, then on every foll 4th row until 28 (29: 31: 32: 34) sts rem.
Work 7 rows, ending with chart row 186 (190: 194: 198: 202).
Shape shoulder
Keeping chart correct, cast off 9 (10: 10: 11: 11) sts at beg of next and foll alt row.
Work 1 row. Cast off rem 10 (9: 11: 10: 12) sts.

RIGHT FRONT
Cast on 76 (80: 84: 88: 92) sts using 2¼mm (US 1) needles and yarn A.
Row 1 (RS): *P1, K1, rep from * to end.
Row 2: *K1, P1, rep from * to end.
These 2 rows form moss st.
Work in moss st for a further 10 rows, ending with a WS row.
Join in yarn B.
Row 13 (RS): Using yarn A (P1, K1) 3 times, *using yarn B K1, using yarn A K1, rep from * to end.
Break off yarn B.
Work in moss st for a further 12 rows, ending with a RS row.
Next row (WS): P to last 16 sts and turn, leaving rem 16 sts on a holder. 60 (64: 68: 72: 76) sts.
Change to 3mm (US 2/3) needles.
Starting and ending rows as indicated, cont in patt foll chart for fronts and complete to match left front, reversing shapings.

SLEEVES (both alike)
Cast on 65 (65: 67: 69: 69) sts using 2¼mm (US 1) needles and yarn A.
Work in moss st as given for back for 12 rows, inc 1 st at each end of 11th of these rows and ending with a WS row. 67 (67: 69: 71: 71) sts.
Join in yarn B.
Row 13 (RS): Using yarn B K1, *using yarn A K1, using yarn B K1, rep from * to end.
Break off yarn B.

Work in moss st for a further 12 rows, inc 1 st at each end of 8th of these rows and ending with a RS row. 69 (69: 71: 73: 73) sts.
Purl 1 row.
Change to 3mm (US 2/3) needles.
Starting and ending rows as indicated, cont in patt foll chart for sleeves as folls:
Inc 1 st at each end of chart row 5 and every foll 10th row to 89 (97: 99: 101: 93) sts, then on every foll 12th (-: -: -: 8th) row until there are 95 (-: -: -: 103) sts.
Cont straight until chart row 150 (150: 154: 154: 154) has been completed, ending with a WS row.
Shape top
Keeping chart correct, cast off 5 (6: 6: 7: 7) sts at beg of next 2 rows. 85 (85: 87: 87: 89) sts.
Dec 1 st at each end of next 5 rows, then on foll 3 alt rows, then on every foll 4th row until 57 (57: 59: 59: 61) sts rem.
Work 1 row, ending with a WS row.
Dec 1 st at each end of next and foll 6 (6: 7: 7: 8) alt rows, then on foll 3 rows. 37 sts.
Cast off 4 sts at beg of next 2 rows.
Cast off rem 29 sts.

MAKING UP
PRESS all pieces as described on the info page.
Join shoulder seams using back stitch, or mattress stitch if preferred.
Button border
Slip 16 sts left on left front holder onto 2¼mm (US 1) needles and rejoin yarn A with RS facing.
Cont in moss st as set until border, when slightly stretched, fits up left front opening edge to neck shaping, ending with a WS row.
Break yarn and leave sts on a holder.
Slip st border in place.
Mark positions for 6 buttons on this border – first to come in first row of border, last to come 6 cm down from neck shaping and rem 4 buttons evenly spaced between.
Buttonhole border
Work to match button border, rejoining yarn with WS facing and with the addition of 6 buttonholes worked to correspond with positions marked for buttons as folls:
Next row (buttonhole row) (RS): Moss st 6 sts, work 2 tog, yrn, moss st 8 sts.
When border is complete, end with a WS row, do NOT break off yarn. Slip st border in place.
Neckband
With RS facing, 2¼mm (US 1) needles and yarn A, moss st 16 sts of buttonhole border, pick up and knit 32 (33: 33: 36: 36) sts up right side of neck, 43 (45: 45: 47: 47) sts from back, and 32 (33: 33: 36: 36) sts down left side of neck, then moss st 16 sts of button border. 139 (143: 143: 151: 151) sts.
Work in moss st as set by front borders for 5 rows, ending with a WS row.
Join in yarn B.
Next row (buttonhole row) (RS): Using yarn A moss st 6 sts, work 2 tog, yrn, *using yarn B K1, using yarn A K1, rep from * to last 5 sts, using yarn A (P1, K1) twice, P1.
Break off yarn B. Work in moss st for a further 5 rows. Cast off in moss st.
Using diagram as a guide, embroider stems on each leaf motif using yarn D.
See information page for finishing instructions, setting in sleeves using the set-in method.

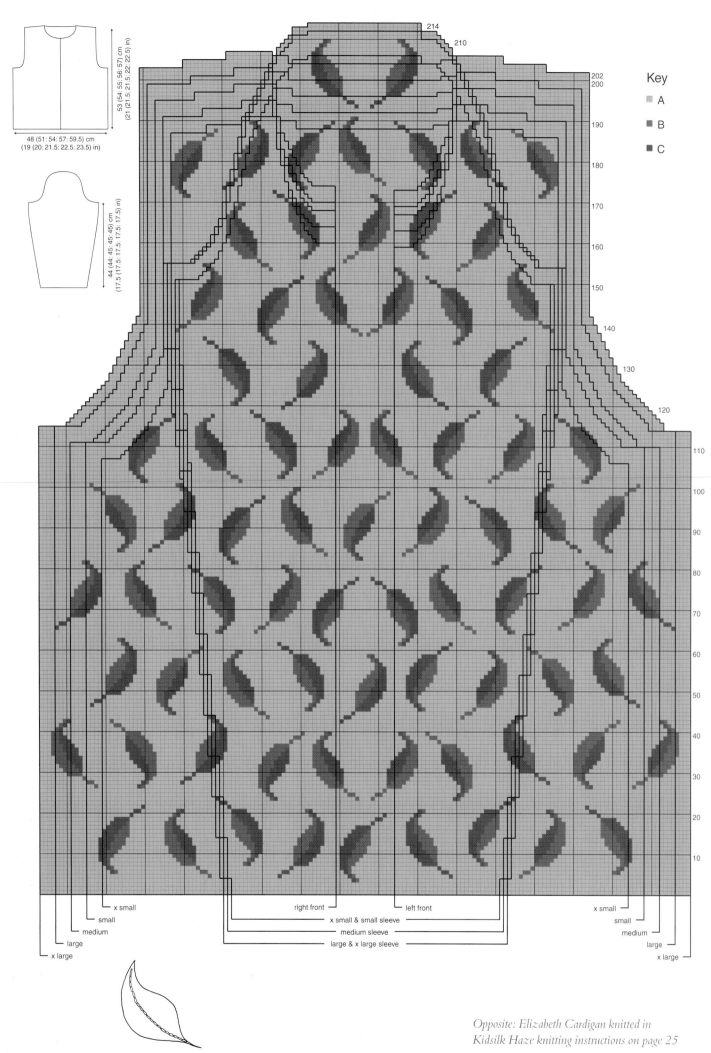

53 (54: 55: 56: 57) cm
(21 (21.5: 21.5: 22: 22.5) in)

48 (51: 54: 57: 59.5) cm
(19 (20: 21.5: 22.5: 23.5) in)

44 (44: 45: 45: 45) cm
(17.5 (17.5: 17.5: 17.5: 17.5) in)

214
210
202
200
190
180
170
160
150
140
130
120
110
100
90
80
70
60
50
40
30
20
10

Key
A
B
C

x small
small
medium
large
x large

right front
x small & small sleeve
medium sleeve
large & x large sleeve

left front

x small
small
medium
large
x large

Opposite: Elizabeth Cardigan knitted in
Kidsilk Haze knitting instructions on page 25

22

ELIZABETH

YARN

Rowan Kidsilk Haze

	XS	S	M	L	XL		
To fit bust	81	86	91	97	102	cm	
	32	34	36	38	40	in	

Polo neck sweater

	5	5	5	6	6	x	25gm

Round neck sweater

	5	5	5	6	6	x	25gm

Cardigan

	5	5	5	6	6	x	25gm

Cardigan only: 1 ball of same yarn in contrast colour for edging
(round neck sweater photographed in Toffee 598, polo neck sweater in Heavenly 592, cardigan in Poison 594 and Lord 593)

NEEDLES

1 pair 2¾mm (no 12) (US 2) needles
1 pair 3¼mm (no 10) (US 3) needles
2¾mm (no 12) (US 2) circular needle

BUTTONS

9 for cardigan

BEADS

BEADS (optional) – **round neck sweater only**: approx 1,400 beads

TENSION

25 sts and 34 rows to 10 cm measured over stocking stitch using 3¼mm (US 3) needles.

Polo neck sweater

BACK

Cast on 441 (465: 489: 513: 537) sts using 2¾mm (US 2) circular needle.
**Row 1 (RS): K1, *K2, lift first of these 2 sts now on right needle over 2nd st and off right needle, rep from * to end.
Row 2: Purl.
Rep rows 1 and 2 once more.
111 (117: 123: 129: 135) sts.
These 4 rows form frill edging.
Change to 3¼mm (US 3) needles.*******
Beg with a K row, work in st st for 18 (20: 20: 22: 22) rows, ending with a WS row.
****Counting in from both ends of last row, place marker on 27th (29th: 31st: 33rd: 35th) sts in from side seam edges.
Next row (RS) (dec): K2tog, *K to within 2 sts of marked st, K2tog, K marked st, K2tog tbl, rep from * once more, K to last 2 sts, K2tog.
Work 13 rows.
Rep last 14 rows once more and then first of these rows (the dec row) again.
93 (99: 105: 111: 117) sts.
Work 19 rows, ending with a WS row.
Next row (RS) (inc): Inc in first st, *K to marker, M1, K marked st, M1, rep from * once more, K to last st, inc in last st.
Work 17 rows.
Rep last 18 rows once more and then first of these rows (the inc row) again.
111 (117: 123: 129: 135) sts.

Cont straight until back measures 37 (38: 38: 39: 39) cm, ending with a WS row.
Shape armholes
Cast off 5 (6: 6: 7: 7) sts at beg of next 2 rows.
101 (105: 111: 115: 121) sts.
Dec 1 st at each end of next 5 (5: 7: 7: 9) rows, then on foll 7 (8: 8: 9: 9) alt rows.
77 (79: 81: 83: 85) sts.
Cont straight until armhole measures 20 (20: 21: 21: 22) cm, ending with a WS row.
Shape shoulders and back neck
Cast off 6 (6: 7: 7: 7) sts at beg of next 2 rows.
65 (67: 67: 69: 71) sts.
Next row (RS): Cast off 6 (6: 7: 7: 7) sts, K until there are 11 (11: 10: 10: 11) sts on right needle and turn, leaving rem sts on a holder.
Work each side of neck separately.
Cast off 4 sts at beg of next row.
Cast off rem 7 (7: 6: 6: 7) sts.
With RS facing, rejoin yarn to rem sts, cast off centre 31 (33: 33: 35: 35) sts, K to end.
Work to match first side, reversing shapings.

FRONT

Work as given for back until 20 (20: 20: 22: 22) rows less have been worked to start of shoulder shaping, ending with a WS row.
Shape neck
Next row (RS): K27 (27: 28: 29: 30) and turn, leaving rem sts on a holder.
Work each side of neck separately.
Dec 1 st at neck edge on next 4 rows, then on foll 3 (3: 3: 4: 4) alt rows, then on foll 4th row.
19 (19: 20: 20: 21) sts.
Work 5 rows, ending with a WS row.
Shape shoulder
Cast off 6 (6: 7: 7: 7) sts at beg of next and foll alt row.
Work 1 row.
Cast off rem 7 (7: 6: 6: 7) sts.
With RS facing, rejoin yarn to rem sts, cast off centre 23 (25: 25: 25: 25) sts, K to end.
Work to match first side, reversing shapings.

44.5 (47: 49: 51.5: 54) cm
(17.5 (18.5: 19.5: 20.5: 21.5) in)

57 (58: 59: 60: 61) cm
(22.5 (23: 23: 23.5: 24) in)

46 (46: 47: 47: 47) cm
(18 (18: 18.5: 18.5: 18.5) in)

SLEEVES (both alike)

Cast on 201 (201: 209: 217: 217) sts using 2¾mm (US 2) circular needle.
**Row 1 (RS): K1, *K2, lift first of these 2 sts now on right needle over 2nd st and off right needle, rep from * to end.
Row 2: Purl.
Rep rows 1 and 2 once more.
51 (51: 53: 55: 55) sts.
These 4 rows form frill edging.
Change to 3¼mm (US 3) needles.*******
Beg with a K row, work in st st, shaping sides by inc 1 st at each end of 11th and every foll 10th row to 71 (63: 67: 69: 61) sts, then on every foll 8th row until there are 81 (83: 85: 87: 89) sts.
****Cont straight until sleeve measures 46 (46: 47: 47: 47) cm, ending with a WS row.
Shape top
Cast off 5 (6: 6: 7: 7) sts at beg of next 2 rows.
71 (71: 73: 73: 75) sts.
Dec 1 st at each end of next 3 rows, then on foll 3 alt rows, then on every foll 4th row until 45 (45: 47: 47: 49) sts rem.
Work 1 row, ending with a WS row.
Dec 1 st at each end of next and foll 2 (2: 3: 3: 4) alt rows, then on foll 3 rows. Cast off rem 33 sts.

Round neck sweater

Beading note: Beads are optional. If using beads, thread them onto yarn before beginning, threading approx 250 beads onto first ball. Place beads within knitting as folls: bring yarn to front (RS) of work and slip next st purlwise, slide bead along yarn so that it sits in front of st just slipped, then take yarn to back (WS) of work. For unbeaded version, work as given for beaded version replacing "bead 1" with "K1".

BACK

Work as given for back of polo neck sweater to *******.
Work in bead patt as folls:
Beg with a K row, work in st st for 6 rows.
Row 7 (RS): K4, *place bead (see beading note), K5, rep from * to last 5 sts, place bead, K4.
Beg with a P row, work in st st for 7 rows.
Row 15 (RS): K1, *place bead (see beading note), K5, rep from * to last 2 sts, place bead, K1.
Row 16: Purl.
These 16 rows form bead patt.
Work in bead patt for a further 2 (4: 4: 6: 6) rows, ending with a WS row.
Keeping bead patt correct throughout, work as given for back of polo neck sweater from ******** to start of shoulder shaping, ending with a WS row.
Shape shoulders and back neck
Cast off 5 sts at beg of next 2 rows.
67 (69: 71: 73: 75) sts.
Next row (RS): Cast off 5 sts, patt until there are 8 (8: 9: 9: 10) sts on right needle and turn, leaving rem sts on a holder.
Work each side of neck separately.
Cast off 4 sts at beg of next row.
Cast off rem 4 (4: 5: 5: 6) sts.
With RS facing, rejoin yarn to rem sts, cast off centre 41 (43: 43: 45: 45) sts, patt to end.
Work to match first side, reversing shapings.

(Knitting instructions continued on page 85)

Opposite: Elizabeth Round Neck Sweater knitted in Kidsilk Haze

PAISLEY

YARN

Rowan Felted Tweed or Kidsilk Haze

	XS	S	M	L	XL
To fit bust	81	86	91	97	102 cm
	32	34	36	38	40 in

Single polo neck sweater with long sleeves
Felted Tweed   6   6   7   7   8 x 50gm
(photographed in Melody 142)

Scooped neck sweater with ¾ sleeves
Kidsilk Haze★   8   9   10   10   11 x 25gm
(photographed in Liqueur 595)
★ Use Kidsilk Haze **DOUBLE** throughout.

NEEDLES

1 pair 3mm (no 11) (US 2/3) needles
1 pair 3¾mm (no 9) (US 5) needles

TENSION

23 sts and 32 rows to 10 cm measured over
stocking stitch using 3¾mm (US 5) needles and
either 1 strand of Felted Tweed **or** 2 strands of
Kidsilk Haze held together.

Shaping note:

All **side seam decreases** are worked 2 sts in
from ends of rows. To dec 1 st at beg of rows
work: K2, K2tog, K to end. To dec 1 st at end of
rows work: K to last 4 sts, K2tog tbl, K2.
All **side seam and sleeve increases** are
worked 2 sts in from ends of rows. To inc 1 st at
beg of rows work: K2, M1, K to end. To inc 1 st
at end of rows work: K to last 2 sts, M1, K2.

Single polo neck sweater
BACK

Cast on 99 (105: 111: 117: 123) sts using 3mm
(US 2/3) needles.
Row 1 (RS): P3, ★K3, P3, rep from ★ to end.
Row 2: K3, ★P3, K3, rep from ★ to end.
These 2 rows form rib.
Work a further 12 rows in rib, ending with a
WS row.
Change to 3¾mm (US 5) needles and beg with
a K row, cont in st st as folls:
Work 8 (10: 10: 12: 12) rows, ending with a WS
row.
Dec 1 st at each end of next and every foll 6th row
until 93 (99: 105: 111: 117) sts rem, then on every
foll 4th row until 83 (89: 95: 101: 107) sts rem.
Work 11 (11: 11: 13: 13) rows, ending with a WS
row.★★
Inc 1 st at each end of next and every foll 6th
row until there are 99 (105: 111: 117: 123) sts.
Work 13 rows, ending with a WS row. (Back
should measure approx 38 (39: 39: 40: 40) cm.)
Shape armholes
Cast off 4 sts at beg of next 2 rows.
91 (97: 103: 109: 115) sts.
Dec 1 st at each end of next 3 (5: 5: 5: 5) rows, then
on every foll alt row until 75 (77: 83: 89: 95) sts rem.
Cont straight until armhole measures 20 (20: 21:
21: 22) cm, ending with a WS row.
Shape shoulders and back neck
Cast off 7 (7: 8: 9: 10) sts at beg of next 2 rows.
61 (63: 67: 71: 75) sts.
Next row (RS): Cast off 7 (7: 8: 9: 10) sts, K
until there are 11 (11: 12: 12: 13) sts on right
needle and turn, leaving rem sts on a holder.

Work each side of neck separately.
Cast off 4 sts at beg of next row.
Cast off rem 7 (7: 8: 8: 9) sts.
With RS facing, rejoin yarn to rem sts, cast off
centre 25 (27: 27: 29: 29) sts, K to end.
Work to match first side, reversing shapings.

FRONT
Work as given for back until 22 (22: 22: 24: 24)
rows less have been worked than on back to start
of shoulder shaping, ending with a WS row.
Shape neck
Next row (RS): K32 (32: 35: 38: 41) and turn,
leaving rem sts on a holder.
Work each side of neck separately.
Cast off 4 sts at beg of next row.
28 (28: 31: 34: 37) sts.
Dec 1 st at neck edge on next 3 rows, then on
foll 2 (2: 2: 3: 3) alt rows, then on every foll 4th
row until 21 (21: 24: 26: 29) sts rem.
Work 5 rows, ending with a RS row.
Shape shoulder
Cast off 7 (7: 8: 9: 10) sts at beg of next and foll
alt row.
Work 1 row.
Cast off rem 7 (7: 8: 8: 9) sts.
With RS facing, rejoin yarn to rem sts, cast off
centre 11 (13: 13: 13: 13) sts, K to end.
Work to match first side, reversing shapings.

SLEEVES (both alike)
Cast on 45 (47: 49: 51: 53) sts using 3mm (US
2/3) needles.
Row 1 (RS): K0 (1: 2: 0: 1), P3, ★K3, P3, rep
from ★ to last 0 (1: 2: 0: 1) sts, K0 (1: 2: 0: 1).
Row 2: P0 (1: 2: 0: 1), K3, ★P3, K3, rep from ★ to
last 0 (1: 2: 0: 1) sts, P0 (1: 2: 0: 1).
These 2 rows form rib.

58 (59: 60: 61: 62) cm
(23: 23: 23.5: 24: 24.5) in

43 (45.5: 48.5: 51: 53.5) cm
(17 (18: 19: 20: 21) in)

41 (41: 42: 42: 42) cm
(16 (16: 16.5: 16.5: 16.5) in)

32 (32: 33: 33: 33) cm
(12.5 (12.5: 13: 13: 13) in)

Work a further 12 rows in rib, inc 1 st at each
end of 9th of these rows. 47 (49: 51: 53: 55) sts.
Change to 3¾mm (US 5) needles and beg with
a K row, cont in st st as folls:
Work 6 rows, ending with a WS row.
Inc 1 st at each end of next and every foll 10th
row until there are 53 (55: 59: 61: 63) sts, then
on every foll 8th row until there are 73 (75: 77:
79: 81) sts.
Cont straight until sleeve measures 41 (41: 42: 42:
42) cm from cast-on edge, ending with a WS row.
Shape top
Cast off 4 (4: 5: 5: 6) sts at beg of next 2 rows.
65 (67: 67: 69: 69) sts.
Dec 1 st at each end of next 5 rows, then on foll
3 alt rows, then on every foll 4th row until
39 (41: 39: 41: 39) sts rem.
Work 1 row.
Dec 1 st at each end of next and foll 0 (1: 0: 1: 0)
alt rows, then on foll 3 rows, ending with a WS
row. 31 sts.
Cast off 4 sts at beg of next 4 rows.
Cast off rem 15 sts.

Scooped neck sweater
BACK
Work as given for back of single polo neck sweater.

FRONT
Work as given for back of single polo neck
sweater to ★★.
Inc 1 st at each end of next and every foll 6th
row until there are 95 (101: 107: 113: 119) sts.
Work 1 row, ending with a WS row.
Shape neck
Next row (RS): K44 (47: 50: 53: 56) and turn,
leaving rem sts on a holder.
Work each side of neck separately.
Dec 1 st at neck edge of next 2 rows.
42 (45: 48: 51: 54) sts.
Work 1 row, ending with a WS row.
Dec 1 st at neck edge of next and foll 6th row
and at same time inc 1 st at side seam edge of
next and foll 6th row. 42 (45: 48: 51: 54) sts.
Dec 1 st at neck edge of every foll 6th row from
previous dec until 40 (43: 46: 49: 52) sts rem.
Work 1 row, ending with a WS row.
Shape armhole
Cast off 4 sts at beg of next row.
36 (39: 42: 45: 48) sts.
Work 1 row.
Dec 1 st at armhole edge of next 3 (5: 5: 5: 5) rows,
then on foll 5 alt rows **and at same time** dec
1 st at neck edge of 3rd and every foll 6th row.
26 (26: 29: 32: 35) sts rem.
Dec 1 st at neck edge **only** on every foll 6th
row from previous dec until 21 (21: 24: 26: 29)
sts rem.
Cont straight until front matches back to start of
shoulder shaping, ending with a WS row.
Shape shoulder
Cast off 7 (7: 8: 9: 10) sts at beg of next and foll
alt row.
Work 1 row. Cast off rem 7 (7: 8: 8: 9) sts.
With RS facing, rejoin yarn to rem sts, cast off
centre 7 sts, K to end.
Work to match first side, reversing shapings.

(Knitting instructions continued on page 29)

PAISLEY

(Continued from page 26)

SLEEVES (both alike)
Cast on 51 (53: 55: 57: 59) sts using 3mm (US 2/3) needles.
Row 1 (RS): P0 (1: 2: 0: 1), K3, ★P3, K3, rep from ★ to last 0 (1: 2: 0: 1) sts, P0 (1: 2: 0: 1).
Row 2: K0 (1: 2: 0: 1), P3, ★K3, P3, rep from ★ to last 0 (1: 2: 0: 1) sts, K0 (1: 2: 0: 1).
These 2 rows form rib.
Work a further 12 rows in rib, inc 1 st at each end of 9th of these rows. 53 (55: 57: 59: 61) sts.
Change to 3¾mm (US 5) needles and beg with a K row, cont in st st as folls:
Work 4 rows, ending with a WS row.
Inc 1 st at each end of next and every foll 8th row until there are 73 (75: 77: 79: 81) sts.
Cont straight until sleeve measures 32 (32: 33: 33: 33) cm from cast-on edge, ending with a WS row.
Shape top
Cast off 4 (4: 5: 5: 6) sts at beg of next 2 rows. 65 (67: 67: 69: 69) sts.

Opposite: Paisley Scooped Neck Sweater knitted in Kidsilk Haze, knitting instructions on page 26

Dec 1 st at each end of next 5 rows, then on foll 3 alt rows, then on every foll 4th row until 39 (41: 39: 41: 39) sts rem. Work 1 row.
Dec 1 st at each end of next and foll 0 (1: 0: 1: 0) alt rows, then on foll 3 rows, ending with a WS row. 31 sts.
Cast off 4 sts at beg of next 4 rows. Cast off rem 15 sts.

MAKING UP
PRESS all pieces as described on the info page.
Single polo neck sweater
Join right shoulder seam using back stitch, or mattress stitch if preferred.
Neckband
With RS facing and 3mm (US 2/3) needles, pick up and knit 28 (29: 29: 31: 31) sts down left side of front neck, 11 (13: 13: 13: 13) sts from front, 28 (29: 29: 31: 31) sts up right side of front neck, and 32 (34: 34: 36: 36) sts from back. 99 (105: 105: 111: 111) sts.

Beg with row 2, work in rib as given for back for 9 cm.
Cast off in rib.
Scooped neck sweater
Join shoulder seams using back stitch, or mattress stitch if preferred.
Collar
Cast on 39 sts using 3mm (US 2/3) needles.
Row 1 (RS): K3, ★P3, K3, rep from ★ to end.
Row 2: P3, ★K3, P3, rep from ★ to end.
These 2 rows form rib.
Cont in rib until collar fits around entire neck edge.
Cast off in rib.
Join cast-off and cast-on ends of collar to form a tube, then sew one edge of collar to neck edge, positioning collar seam at centre back neck.
Both sweaters
See information page for finishing instructions, setting in sleeves using the set-in method.

RUMMY SCARF

YARN
Rowan Kid Classic

A Royal	835	2	x	50gm
B Imp	829	2	x	50gm
C Glacier	822	2	x	50gm

Use all yarns **DOUBLE** throughout.

NEEDLES
1 pair 9mm (no 00) (US 13) needles

TENSION
13 sts and 19 rows to 10 cm measured over rib using 9mm (US 13) needles and **two strands of yarn** held together.

FINISHED SIZE
Completed scarf is approx 25 cm (9½ in) by 140 cm (55 in), including fringe.

Scarf
From yarn A, cut 36 lengths of yarn, each 30 cm long, for fringe. Cut same lengths of yarn from yarn C and set all these lengths of yarn to one side.
Using 9mm (US 13) needles cast on 34 sts using yarn A.
Row 1 (RS): K2, (K6, P6) twice, K8.
Row 2: K2, (P6, K6) twice, P6, K2.
These 2 rows form rib.

Cont in rib until almost all of yarn A has been used up, ending with a WS row and leaving sufficient yarn to work another 8 rows (approx 8 m).
Join in yarn B.
Using yarn B, rib 2 rows.
Using yarn A, rib 2 rows.
Rep last 4 rows 3 times more.
Break off yarn A and cont using yarn B only.
Cont in rib until almost all of yarn B has been used up, ending with a WS row and leaving sufficient yarn to work another 8 rows (approx 8 m).
Join in yarn C.
Using yarn C, rib 2 rows.
Using yarn B, rib 2 rows.
Rep last 4 rows 3 times more.
Break off yarn B and cont using yarn C only.
Cont in rib until almost all of yarn C has been used up, ending with a WS row and leaving sufficient yarn to work cast-off row.
Cast off in rib.

MAKING UP
PRESS as described on the information page.
Using colour of yarn to match knitted section, knot pairs of lengths of yarn across both ends of scarf to form fringe as folls: knot first pair through edge st, next pair between 2nd and 3rd sts, then each following pair between every other st, knotting last pair through st at opposite edge.

HUGH

YARN

Rowan Rowanspun Aran or Rowanspun DK

	ladies			mens		
	S	M	L	M	L	XL
To fit bust/chest	86	91	97	102	107	112	cm
	34	36	38	40	42	44	in

Rowan Rowanspun Aran

| | 8 | 9 | 9 | 10 | 10 | 10 x 100gm |

Rowan Rowanspun DK★

| A Eau de Nil 735 | 8 | 9 | 9 | 10 | 10 | 10 x 50gm |
| B Cloud 743 | 8 | 9 | 9 | 10 | 10 | 10 x 50gm |

★ Use **2 strands** of Rowanspun DK (one strand of each colour) held together throughout.

NEEDLES

1 pair 5mm (no 6) (US 8) needles
1 pair 5½mm (no 5) (US 9) needles
Cable needle

TENSION

16 sts and 23 rows to 10 cm measured over stocking stitch using 5½mm (US 9) needles and either **one strand** of Rowanspun Aran, or **two strands** of Rowanspun DK (one strand of each colour) held together.

Pattern note: The pattern is written for the 3 ladies sizes, followed by the 3 mens sizes in **bold**. Where only one figure appears this applies to all sizes in that group.

SPECIAL ABBREVIATIONS

C8B = Cable 8 back Slip next 4 sts onto cable needle and leave at back of work, K4, then K4 from cable needle.
C8F = Cable 8 front Slip next 4 sts onto cable needle and leave at front of work, K4, then K4 from cable needle.

BACK

Cast on 108 (112: 116: **124: 128: 132**) sts using 5mm (US 8) needles.
Row 1 (RS): K0 (2: 0: **0: 3: 0**), P3 (3: 0: **4: 3: 1**), (K4, P3) 3 (3: 4: **4: 4: 5**) times, (K8, P3) twice, K16, (P3, K8) twice, (P3, K4) 3 (3: 4: **4: 4: 5**) times, P3 (3: 0: **4: 3: 1**), K0 (2: 0: **0: 3: 0**).
Row 2: P0 (2: 0: **0: 3: 0**), K3 (3: 0: **4: 3: 1**), (P4, K3) 3 (3: 4: **4: 4: 5**) times, (P8, K3) twice, P16, (K3, P8) twice, (K3, P4) 3 (3: 4: **4: 4: 5**) times, K3 (3: 0: **4: 3: 1**), P0 (2: 0: **0: 3: 0**).
These 2 rows form rib.
Work in rib for a further 9 rows, ending with a RS row.
Row 12 (WS) (inc): P0 (2: 0: **0: 3: 0**), K3 (3: 0: **4: 3: 1**), (P4, K3) 3 (3: 4: **4: 4: 5**) times, (P8, M1, K3, M1) twice, P16, (M1, K3, M1, P8) twice, (K3, P4) 3 (3: 4: **4: 4: 5**) times, K3 (3: 0: **4: 3: 1**), P0 (2: 0: **0: 3: 0**). 116 (120: 124: **132: 136: 140**) sts.

Opposite, from left to right: Hugh knitted in Rowanspun DK, Bonny knitted in Rowan Felted Tweed, knitting instructions on page 18, Fin Beret knitted in Kidsilk Haze, knitting instructions on page 77 & Cameron knitted in Rowanspun Aran, knitting instructions on page 8

Change to 5½mm (US 9) needles and cont in cable patt as folls:
Row 1 (RS): P24 (26: 28: **32: 34: 36**), (K8, P5) twice, K16, (P5, K8) twice, P24 (26: 28: **32: 34: 36**).
Row 2: K24 (26: 28: **32: 34: 36**), (P8, K5) twice, P16, (K5, P8) twice, K24 (26: 28: **32: 34: 36**).
Row 3: P24 (26: 28: **32: 34: 36**), (C8B, P5) twice, C8B, C8F, (P5, C8F) twice, P24 (26: 28: **32: 34: 36**).
Row 4: As row 2.
Rows 5 to 14: As rows 1 and 2, 5 times.
These 14 rows form cable patt.
Cont straight until back measures 45 (**40**) cm, ending with a WS row.
Shape armholes
Keeping patt correct, cast off 4 sts at beg of next 2 rows.
108 (112: 116: **124: 128: 132**) sts.
Dec 1 st at each end of next 4 rows.
100 (104: 108: **116: 120: 124**) sts.
Cont straight until armhole measures 25 (26: 27: **28: 29: 30**) cm, ending with a WS row.
Shape shoulders and back neck
Keeping patt correct, cast off 9 (9: 10: **11: 11: 12**) sts at beg of next 2 rows.
82 (86: 88: **94: 98: 100**) sts.
Next row (RS): Cast off 9 (9: 10: **11: 11: 12**) sts, patt until there are 12 (14: 14: **14: 16: 16**) sts on right needle and turn, leaving rem sts on a holder.
Work each side of neck separately.
Cast off 4 sts at beg of next row.
Cast off rem 8 (10: 10: **10: 12: 12**) sts.
With RS facing, rejoin yarn to rem sts, cast off centre 40 (**44**) sts, patt to end.
Work to match first side, reversing shapings.

FRONT

Work as given for back until 16 rows less have been worked to start of shoulder shaping, ending with a WS row.
Shape neck
Next row (RS): Patt 36 (38: 40: **44: 46: 48**) sts and turn, leaving rem sts on a holder.
Work each side of neck separately.
Cast off 4 sts at beg of next row.
32 (34: 36: **40: 42: 44**) sts.
Dec 1 st at neck edge on next 3 (**5**) rows, then on foll 3 alt rows.
26 (28: 30: **32: 34: 36**) sts.
Work 5 (**3**) rows, ending with a WS row.
Shape shoulder
Keeping patt correct, cast off 9 (9: 10: **11: 11: 12**) sts at beg of next and foll alt row.
Work 1 row.
Cast off rem 8 (10: 10: **10: 12: 12**) sts.
With RS facing, rejoin yarn to rem sts, cast off centre 28 sts, patt to end.
Work to match first side, reversing shapings.

SLEEVES (both alike)

Cast on 44 (**54**) sts using 5mm (US 8) needles.
Row 1 (RS): K3 (**1**), ★P3, K4, rep from ★ to last 6 (**4**) sts, P3, K3 (**1**).
Row 2: P3 (**1**), ★K3, P4, rep from ★ to last 6 (**4**) sts, K3, P3 (**1**).
These 2 rows form rib.
Work in rib for a further 10 rows, inc 1 st at each end of 7th of these rows and ending with a WS row. 46 (**56**) sts.

Change to 5½mm (US 9) needles.
Beg with a P row, cont in rev st st, shaping sides by inc 1 st at each end of 3rd and every foll 6th row to 64 (56: 52: **84: 80: 72**) sts, then on every foll 4th row until there are 80 (84: 86: **90: 92: 96**) sts.
Cont straight until sleeve measures 45 (**49**) cm, ending with a WS row.
Shape top
Cast off 4 sts at beg of next 2 rows.
72 (76: 78: **82: 84: 88**) sts.
Dec 1 st at each end of next and foll 4 alt rows.
Work 1 row, ending with a WS row.
Cast off rem 62 (66: 68: **72: 74: 78**) sts.

MAKING UP

PRESS all pieces as described on the info page.
Join right shoulder seam using back stitch, or mattress stitch if preferred.
Collar
With RS facing and 5mm (US 8) needles, pick up and knit 17 (**19**) sts down left side of neck, 17 sts from front, 17 (**19**) sts up right side of neck, then 28 (**31**) sts from back. 79 (**86**) sts.
Row 1 (WS): K1, ★K3, P4, rep from ★ to last st, P1.
Row 2: K1, ★K4, P3, rep from ★ to last st, P1.
Rep these 2 rows until collar measures 11 cm.
Cast off in rib.
See information page for finishing instructions, setting in sleeves using the shallow set-in method.

57.5 (60: 62.5: **67.5: 70: 72.5**) cm
(22.5 (23.5: 24.5: **26.5: 27.5: 28.5**) in)

70 (71: 72: **68: 69: 70**) cm
(27.5 (28: 28.5: **27: 27: 27.5**) in)

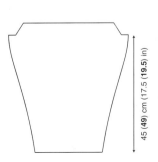

45 (**49**) cm (17.5 (**19.5**) in)

FIRTH

YARN
Rowan Kid Classic

To fit age	6-7	8-9	10-11	12-13 years

One colour jacket

	5	5	6	7	x 50gm

Fairisle jacket

A Bewitch 830	4	4	5	6	x 50gm
B Smoke 831	1	1	1	1	x 50gm
C Cr. Velvet 825	1	1	1	1	x 50gm
D Feather 828	1	1	1	1	x 50gm
E Royal 835	1	1	1	1	x 50gm
F Cherish 833	1	1	1	1	x 50gm

	ladies			mens		
	S	M	L	M	L	XL
To fit bust/chest	86	91	97	102	107	112	cm
	34	36	38	40	42	44	in

One colour jacket

	7	8	8	10	10	11	x 50gm

(mans jacket photographed in Reed 823)

Fairisle jacket

A Imp	829	6	7	7	9	9	10	x 50gm
B Swirl	834	1	1	1	1	1	1	x 50gm
C Cr. Velvet	825	1	1	1	1	1	1	x 50gm
D Royal	835	1	1	1	2	2	2	x 50gm
E Cherish	833	1	1	1	1	1	1	x 50gm
F Juicy	827	1	1	1	1	1	1	x 50gm

NEEDLES
1 pair 4¹/₂mm (no 7) (US 7) needles
1 pair 5mm (no 6) (US 8) needles
1 pair 5¹/₂mm (no 5) (US 9) needles

ZIP – 31 (36: 36: 41: **46:** 51) cm open-ended zip

TENSION
19 sts and 25 rows to 10 cm measured over stocking stitch using 5mm (US 8) needles.

Pattern note: The pattern is written for the 4 childrens sizes, followed by the 3 ladies sizes in **bold**, followed by the 3 mens sizes. Where only one figure appears this applies to all sizes in that group.

Fairisle jacket
BACK
Cast on 79 (83: 87: 91: **95: 101: 107:** 115: 121: 127) sts using 4¹/₂mm (US 7) needles and yarn A.
Row 1 (RS): K2 (0: 0: 2: **0: 1: 0:** 2: 0: 2), P3 (1: 3: 3: **1: 3: 1:** 3: 2: 3), *K3, P3, rep from * to last 2 (4: 0: 2: **4: 1: 4:** 2: 5: 2), K2 (3: 0: 2: **3: 1: 3:** 2: 3: 2), P0 (1: 0: 0: **1: 0: 1:** 0: 2: 0).
Row 2: P2 (0: 0: 2: **0: 1: 0:** 2: 0: 2), K3 (1: 3: 3: **1: 3: 1:** 3: 2: 3), *P3, K3, rep from * to last 2 (4: 0: 2: **4: 1: 4:** 2: 5: 2), P2 (3: 0: 2: **3: 1: 3:** 2: 3: 2), K0 (1: 0: 0: **1: 0: 1:** 0: 2: 0).
Rep last 2 rows 5 (**7:** 9) times more.
Change to 5mm (US 8) needles.
Beg with a K row, work in st st until back measures 19 (21: 23: 25: **27:** 35) cm, ending with a WS row.
Shape raglan armholes
Cast off 5 (**6:** 8) sts at beg of next 2 rows.
69 (73: 77: 81: **83: 89: 95:** 99: 105: 111) sts.
Work 0 (0: 0: 4: **1: 2: 2:** 2) rows, dec 1 st at each end of every row.
69 (73: 77: 73: **81: 85: 91:** 95: 101: 107) sts.

Work 0 (**1: 0: 0:** 0) row, ending with a WS row.
Change to 5¹/₂mm (US 9) needles.
Using the **fairisle** technique as described on the information page and starting and ending rows as indicated, cont in patt foll chart for body, which is worked entirely in st st, as folls:
Dec 1 st at each end of next 9 (9: 7: 1: **1: 3: 7: 3:** 7: 11) rows, then on foll 11 (11: 12: 15: **15: 14: 12:** 14: 12: 10) alt rows.
29 (33: 39: 41: **49: 51: 53:** 61: 63: 65) sts.
Work 1 row, completing all 32 rows of chart.
Change to 5mm (US 8) needles.
Cont in st st using yarn A only as folls:
Dec 1 st at each end of next and foll 4 (5: 7: 7: **10: 11**) alt rows. 19 (21: 23: 25: **27: 29: 31:** 37: 39: 41) sts.
Work 1 row, ending with a WS row. Cast off.

LEFT FRONT
Cast on 41 (43: 45: 47: **49: 52: 55:** 59: 62: 65) sts using 4¹/₂mm (US 7) needles and yarn A.
Row 1 (RS): K2 (0: 0: 2: **0: 1: 0:** 2: 0: 2), P3 (1: 3: 3: **1: 3: 1:** 3: 2: 3), *K3, P3, rep from * to last 6 sts, K3, P2, K1.
Row 2: K3, *P3, K3, rep from * to last 2 (4: 0: 2: **4: 1: 4:** 2: 5: 2), P2 (3: 0: 2: **3: 1: 3:** 2: 3: 2), K0 (1: 0: 0: **1: 0: 1:** 0: 2: 0).
Rep last 2 rows 5 (**7:** 9) times more.
Change to 5mm (US 8) needles.
Next row (RS): Knit.
Next row: K1, P to end.
These 2 rows set the sts – front opening edge st worked as a K st on every row and all other sts in st st.
Cont as set until left front matches back to beg of raglan armhole shaping, ending with a WS row.
Shape raglan armholes
Cast off 5 (**6:** 8) sts at beg of next row.
36 (38: 40: 42: **43: 46: 49:** 51: 54: 57).
Work 1 row.
Work 0 (0: 0: 4: **1: 2: 2:** 2) rows, dec 1 st at raglan edge of every row.
36 (38: 40: 38: **42: 44: 47:** 49: 52: 55).
Work 0 (**1: 0: 0:** 0) row, ending with a WS row.
Change to 5¹/₂mm (US 9) needles.
Starting and ending rows as indicated, cont in patt foll chart for body as folls:
Dec 1 st at raglan edge of next 9 (9: 7: 1: **1: 3: 7: 3:** 7: 11) rows, then on foll 11 (11: 12: 15: **15: 14: 12:** 14: 12: 10) alt rows.
16 (18: 21: 22: **26: 27: 28:** 32: 33: 34).
Work 1 row, completing all 32 rows of chart.
Change to 5mm (US 8) needles.
Cont in st st using yarn A only as folls:
Dec 1 st at raglan edge of next and foll 0 (1: 2: 2: **4:** 4) alt rows, ending with a RS row.
15 (16: 18: 19: **21: 22: 23:** 27: 28: 29).
Shape neck
Cast off 8 (9: 8: 9: **9: 10: 11:** 13: 14: 15) sts at beg of next row. 7 (7: 10: 10: **12:** 14).
Dec 1 st at neck edge of next 3 (3: 5: 5: **5:** 5) rows, then on foll 0 (**1:** 2) alt rows **and at same time** dec 1 st at raglan edge on next and every foll alt row. 2 sts.
Work 1 row.
Next row (RS): K2tog and fasten off.

RIGHT FRONT
Cast on 41 (43: 45: 47: **49: 52: 55:** 59: 62: 65) sts using 4¹/₂mm (US 7) needles and yarn A.

Row 1 (RS): K1, P2, *K3, P3, rep from * to last 2 (4: 0: 2: **4: 1: 4:** 2: 5: 2), K2 (3: 0: 2: **3: 1: 3:** 2: 3: 2), P0 (1: 0: 0: **1: 0: 1:** 0: 2: 0).
Row 2: P2 (0: 0: 2: **0: 1: 0:** 2: 0: 2), K3 (1: 3: 3: **1: 3: 1:** 3: 2: 3), *P3, K3, rep from * to end.
Rep last 2 rows 5 (**7:** 9) times more.
Change to 5mm (US 8) needles.
Next row (RS): Knit.
Next row: P to last st, K1.
These 2 rows set the sts – front opening edge st worked as a K st on every row and all other sts in st st.
Complete to match left front, reversing shapings.

SLEEVES (both alike)
Cast on 35 (37: 41: 43: **47:** 61) sts using 4¹/₂mm (US 7) needles and yarn A.
Row 1 (RS): K0 (0: 1: 2: **0:** 0), P1 (2: 3: 3: **1:** 2), *K3, P3, rep from * to last 4 (5: 1: 2: **4:** 5) sts, K3 (3: 1: 2: **3:** 3), P1 (2: 0: 0: **1:** 2).
Row 2: P0 (0: 1: 2: **0:** 0), K1 (2: 3: 3: **1:** 2), *P3, K3, rep from * to last 4 (5: 1: 2: **4:** 5) sts, P3 (3: 1: 2: **3:** 3), K1 (2: 0: 0: **1:** 2).
These 2 rows form rib.
Work in rib for a further 10 (**14:** 18) rows, inc 1 st at each end of 7th (**11th:** 13th) of these rows.
37 (39: 43: 45: **49:** 63) sts.
Change to 5mm (US 8) needles.
Beg with a K row, cont in st st, shaping sides by inc 1 st at each end of 3rd (3rd: 3rd: 5th: **5th: 3rd: 3rd:** 3rd: 3rd: 1st) and every foll 6th (**8th: 6th: 6th:** 8th: 6th: 6th) row to 41 (53: 67: 73: **57: 79: 71:** 71: 97: 97) sts, then on every foll 4th (4th: 4th: -: **6th: 4th: 4th:** 6th: -: 4th) row until there are 63 (65: 69: -: **77: 81: 85:** 95: -: 99) sts.
Cont straight until sleeve measures 30 (34: 38: 42: **45:** 50) cm from cast-on edge, end with a WS row.
Shape raglan armholes
Cast off 5 (**6:** 8) sts at beg of next 2 rows.
53 (55: 59: 63: **65: 69: 73:** 79: 81: 83) sts.
Work 0 (0: 0: 3: **1: 2: 2:** 2) rows, dec 1 st at each end of every row.
53 (55: 59: 57: **63: 65: 69:** 75: 77: 79) sts.
Work 0 (0: 0: 1: **1: 0: 0:** 0) row, end with a WS row.
Change to 5¹/₂mm (US 9) needles.
Starting and ending rows as indicated, cont in patt foll chart for sleeve as folls:
Work 0 (**2: 0: 0:** 0) rows.
Dec 1 st at each end of next 3 (3: 3: 1: **1: 1: 5:** 7: 9: 11) rows, then on foll 14 (14: 14: 15: **14: 15: 13:** 12: 11: 10) alt rows. 19 (21: 25: 25: **33:** 37) sts.
Work 1 row, completing all 32 rows of chart.
Change to 5mm (US 8) needles.
Cont in st st using yarn A only as folls:
Dec 1 st at each end of next and foll 2 (3: 5: 5: **8:** 9) alt rows. 13 (**15:** 17) sts.
Work 1 row, ending with a WS row.
Left sleeve only
Dec 1 st at each end of next row. 11 (**13:** 15) sts.
Cast off 3 (**4:** 4) sts at beg of next row. 8 (**9:** 11) sts.
Dec 1 st at beg of next row. 7 (**8:** 10) sts.
Cast off 4 (**4:** 5) sts at beg of next row. 3 (**4:** 5) sts.
Right sleeve only
Cast off 4 (**5:** 5) sts at beg and dec 1 st at end of next row. 8 (**9:** 11) sts.
Work 1 row. Cast off 4 (**4:** 5) sts at beg and dec 1 st at end of next row. 3 (**4:** 5) sts. Work 1 row.

Opposite: Firth Jackets both knitted in Kid Classic

(Knitting instruction continued on page 34)

33

FIRTH

Continued from page 33

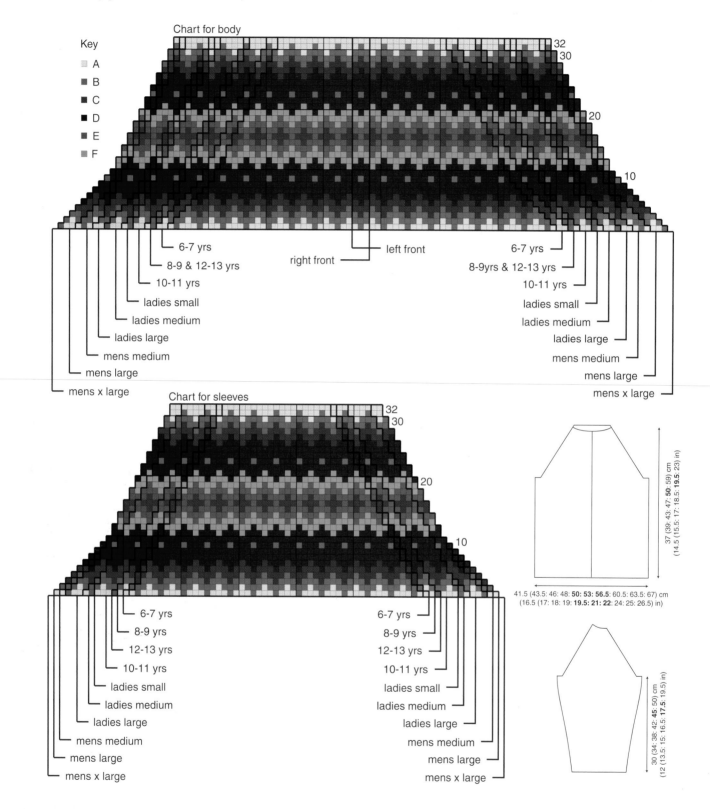

Chart for body

Key

- ☐ A
- ■ B
- ■ C
- ■ D
- ■ E
- ■ F

6-7 yrs
8-9 & 12-13 yrs
10-11 yrs
ladies small
ladies medium
ladies large
mens medium
mens large
mens x large

right front — left front

6-7 yrs
8-9yrs & 12-13 yrs
10-11 yrs
ladies small
ladies medium
ladies large
mens medium
mens large
mens x large

Chart for sleeves

6-7 yrs
8-9 yrs
12-13 yrs
10-11 yrs
ladies small
ladies medium
ladies large
mens medium
mens large
mens x large

6-7 yrs
8-9 yrs
12-13 yrs
10-11 yrs
ladies small
ladies medium
ladies large
mens medium
mens large
mens x large

37 (39: 43: 47: **50: 59**) cm
(14.5 (15.5: 17: 18.5: **19.5: 23**) in)

41.5 (43.5: 46: 48: **50: 53: 56.5**: 60.5: 63.5: 67) cm
(16.5 (17: 18: 19: **19.5: 21: 22**: 24: 25: 26.5) in)

30 (34: 38: 42: **45: 50**) cm
(12 (13.5: 15: 16.5: **17.5**: 19.5) in)

Both sleeves
Cast off rem 3 (**4**: 5) sts.

MAKING UP
PRESS all pieces as described on the info page.
Join raglan seams using back stitch, or mattress
stitch if preferred.
Collar
With RS facing, 4½mm (US 7) needles and yarn
A, starting and ending at front opening edge, pick

up and knit 14 (13: 15: 17: **17: 19: 21**: 25: 27: 26) sts
up right side of neck, 12 (**14**: 16) sts from top of
right sleeve, 19 (21: 23: 25: **27: 29: 31**: 37: 39: 41) sts
from back, 12 (**14**: 16) sts from top of left sleeve,
then 14 (13: 15: 17: **17: 19: 21**: 25: 27: 26) sts
down left side of neck.
71 (71: 77: 83: **89: 95: 101**: 119: 125: 125) sts.
Row 1 (RS of collar, WS of body): (K1, P1)
twice, K3, ★P3, K3, rep from ★ to last 4 sts, (P1,
K1) twice.

Row 2: (K1, P1) twice, P3, ★K3, P3, rep from ★
to last 4 sts, (P1, K1) twice.
Rep these 2 rows until collar measures 8 (10: 12) cm.
Cast off in patt.
See information page for finishing instructions,
inserting zip into front opening.

One colour jacket
Work as given for fairisle jacket but using same
colour throughout.

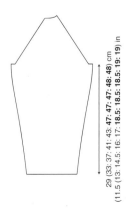

KATIE

YARN

Rowan Rowanspun DK

To fit age	5-6	7-8	9-10	11-12	13-14	years
	4	5	6	6	7	x 50gm
	XS	S	M	L	XL	
To fit bust	81	86	91	97	102	cm
	32	34	36	38	40	in
	7	7	7	8	8	x 50gm

(childs photographed in Punch 731, ladies in Lavender 733)

NEEDLES

1 pair 3¾mm (no 9) (US 5) needles
1 pair 4mm (no 8) (US 6) needles

ZIP – 31 (36: 41: 46: 46: **51**) cm open ended zip

TENSION

21 sts and 29 rows to 10 cm measured over stocking stitch using 4mm (US 6) needles.

Pattern note: The pattern is written for the 5 childrens sizes, followed by the ladies sizes in **bold**. Where only one figure appears this applies to all sizes in that group.

BACK

Cast on 75 (79: 83: 87: 91: **91: 97: 103: 109: 115**) sts using 3¾mm (US 5) needles.
Row 1 (RS): K0 (2: 0: 0: 2: **2: 0: 1: 0: 0**), P3 (3: 1: 3: 3: **3: 1: 3: 0: 3**), ★K3 (**4**), P3, rep from ★ to last 0 (2: 4: 0: 2: **2: 5: 1: 4: 0**) sts, K0 (2: 3: 0: 2: **2: 4: 1: 4: 0**), P0 (0: 1: 0: 0: **0: 1: 0: 0: 0**).
Row 2: P0 (2: 0: 0: 2: **2: 0: 1: 0: 0**), K3 (3: 1: 3: 3: **3: 1: 3: 0: 3**), ★P3 (**4**), K3, rep from ★ to last 0 (2: 4: 0: 2: **2: 5: 1: 4: 0**) sts, P0 (2: 3: 0: 2: **2: 4: 1: 4: 0**), K0 (0: 1: 0: 0: **0: 1: 0: 0: 0**).
Rep last 2 rows 4 (**6**) times more.
Change to 4mm (US 6) needles.
Beg with a K row, cont in st st as folls:
Work 2 (2: 2: 4: 4: **2**) rows.
Next row (RS) (dec): K2, K2tog, K to last 4 sts, K2tog tbl, K2.
Working all decreases 2 sts in from ends of rows as set by last row, cont as folls:
Dec 1 st at each end of every foll 4th (6th: 8th: 6th: 6th: **6th**) row until 67 (71: 75: 77: 79: **79: 85: 91: 97: 103**) sts rem, then on foll – (**4th**) row.
67 (71: 75: 77: 79: **77: 83: 89: 95: 101**) sts.
Work 7 (7: 7: 9: 9: **9**) rows, ending with a WS row.
Next row (RS) (inc): K2, M1, K to last 2 sts, M1, K2.
Working all increases 2 sts in from ends of rows as set by last row, cont as folls:
Inc 1 st at each end of every foll 6th (8th: 10th: 8th: 8th: **6th**) row to 75 (79: 83: 87: 91: **91: 97: 103: 109: 115**) sts, then on every foll – (**4th**) row until there are - (**95: 101: 107: 113: 119**) sts.
Cont straight until back measures 20 (25: 29: 33: 36: **38**) cm, ending with a WS row.
Shape raglan armholes
Cast off 4 (4: 5: 5: 6: **6: 6: 7: 7: 8**) sts at beg of next 2 rows. 67 (71: 73: 77: 79: **83: 89: 93: 99: 103**) sts.

Opposite, from left to right Tippi Sweater knitted in Rowanspun DK (trebled), knitting instructions on page 37 & Katie Jacket knitted in Rowanspun DK

7-8 and 11-12 years and ladies sizes only

Next row (RS): K3, K3tog, K to last 6 sts, K3tog tbl, K3.
Work 1 row.
Rep last 2 rows – (0: –: 0: –: **0: 1: 2: 3: 4**) times more. - (67: –: 73: –: **79: 81: 81: 83: 83**) sts.

All sizes

Next row (RS): K3, K3tog, K to last 6 sts, K3tog tbl, K3.
Work 3 rows.
Rep last 4 rows 10 (10: 11: 11: 12: **12**) times more, and then first 2 of these rows again, ending with a WS row.
Cast off rem 19 (19: 21: 21: 23: **23: 25: 25: 27: 27**) sts.

LEFT FRONT

Cast on 38 (40: 42: 44: 46: **46: 49: 52: 55: 58**) sts using 3¾mm (US 5) needles.
Row 1 (RS): K0 (2: 0: 0: 2: **2: 0: 1: 0: 0**), P3 (3: 1: 3: 3: **3: 1: 3: 0: 3**), ★K3 (**4**), P3, rep from ★ to last 5 (**6**) sts, K3 (**4**), P2.
Row 2: P1, K1, ★P3 (**4**), K3, rep from ★ to last 0 (2: 4: 0: 2: **2: 5: 1: 4: 0**) sts, P0 (2: 3: 0: 2: **2: 4: 1: 4: 0**), K0 (0: 1: 0: 0: **0: 1: 0: 0: 0**).
Rep last 2 rows 4 (**6**) times more.
Change to 4mm (US 6) needles.
Next row (RS): K to last 2 sts, P2.
Next row: P1, K1, P to end.
These 2 rows set the sts.
Keeping sts correct as set, cont as folls:
Work a further 0 (0: 0: 2: 2: **0**) rows.
Next row (RS) (dec): K2, K2tog, K to last 2 sts, P2.
Working all decreases 2 sts in from beg of rows as set by last row, cont as folls:
Dec 1 st at beg of every foll 4th (6th: 8th: 6th: 6th: **6th**) row until 34 (36: 38: 39: 40: **40: 43: 46: 49: 52**) sts rem, then on foll – (**4th**) row.
34 (36: 38: 39: 40: **39: 42: 45: 48: 51**) sts.
Work 7 (7: 7: 9: 9: **9**) rows, ending with a WS row.
Next row (RS) (inc): K2, M1, K to last 2 sts, P2.
Working all increases 2 sts in from beg of rows as set by last row, cont as folls:
Inc 1 st at beg of every foll 6th (8th: 10th: 8th: 8th: **6th**) row to 38 (40: 42: 44: 46: **46: 49: 52: 55: 58**) sts, then on every foll – (**4th**) row until there are - (**48: 51: 54: 57: 60**) sts.
Cont straight until left front matches back to beg of raglan armhole shaping, ending with a WS row.
Shape raglan armhole
Cast off 4 (4: 5: 5: 6: **6: 6: 7: 7: 8**) sts at beg of next row. 34 (36: 37: 39: 40: **42: 45: 47: 50: 52**) sts.
Work 1 row.
Working all raglan decreases 3 sts in from ends of rows as given for back, dec 2 sts at raglan edge of next and foll 0 (1: 0: 1: 0: **1: 2: 3: 4: 5**) alt rows, then on every foll 4th row until 16 (16: 19: 19: 20: **20: 23: 23: 24: 24**) sts rem.
Work 0 (0: 2: 2: 0: **0: 2: 2: 0: 0**) rows, ending with a RS row.
Shape neck
Cast off 6 sts at beg of next row.
10 (10: 13: 13: 14: **14: 17: 17: 18: 18**) sts.
Dec 1 st at neck edge of next 3 rows, then on foll 1 (1: 2: 3: 3: **3: 4: 4: 5: 5**) alt rows **and at same time** dec 2 sts at raglan edge on every foll 4th row from previous dec. 4 sts.
Next row (WS): P4.
Next row: (K2tog) twice.
Next row: P2tog and fasten off.

RIGHT FRONT

Cast on 38 (40: 42: 44: 46: **46: 49: 52: 55: 58**) sts using 3¾mm (US 5) needles.
Row 1 (RS): P2, ★K3 (**4**), P3, rep from ★ to last 0 (2: 4: 0: 2: **2: 5: 1: 4: 0**) sts, K0 (2: 3: 0: 2: **2: 4: 1: 4: 0**), P0 (0: 1: 0: 0: **0: 1: 0: 0: 0**).
Row 2: P0 (2: 0: 0: 2: **2: 0: 1: 0: 0**), K3 (3: 1: 3: 3: **3: 1: 3: 0: 3**), ★P3 (**4**), K3, rep from ★ to last 5 (**6**) sts, P3 (**4**), K1, P1.
Rep last 2 rows 4 (**6**) times more.
Change to 4mm (US 6) needles.
Next row (RS): P2, K to end.
Next row: P to last 2 sts, K1, P1.
These 2 rows set the sts.
Keeping sts correct as set, cont as folls:
Work a further 0 (0: 0: 2: 2: **0**) rows.
Next row (RS) (dec): P2, K to last 4 sts, K2tog tbl, K2.
Working all decreases 2 sts in from ends of rows as set by last row, complete to match left front, reversing shapings.

SLEEVES

Cast on 37 (39: 41: 43: 45: **47: 49: 51: 53: 55**) sts using 3¾mm (US 5) needles.
Row 1 (RS): K2 (0: 0: 0: 0: **1: 2: 3: 0: 0**), P3 (0: 1: 2: 3: **3: 3: 3: 0: 1**), ★K3 (**4**), P3, rep from ★ to last 2 (3: 4: 5: 0: **1: 2: 3: 4: 5**) sts, K2 (3: 3: 3: 0: **1: 2: 3: 4: 4**), P0 (0: 1: 2: 0: **0: 0: 0: 0: 1**).
Row 2: P2 (0: 0: 0: 0: **1: 2: 3: 0: 0**), K3 (0: 1: 2: 3: **3: 3: 3: 0: 1**), ★P3 (**4**), K3, rep from ★ to last 2 (3: 4: 5: 0: **1: 2: 3: 4: 5**) sts, P2 (3: 3: 3: 0: **1: 2: 3: 4: 4**), K0 (0: 1: 2: 0: **0: 0: 0: 0: 1**).
Rep last 2 rows 4 (**6**) times more.

(Knitting instructions continued on page 86)

36 (37.5: 39.5: 41.5: 43.5: **45: 48: 51: 54: 56.5**) cm
(14 (15: 15.5: 16.5: 17: **17.5: 19: 20: 21.5: 22**) in)

37 (42: 47: 52: 55: **58: 59: 59: 60: 61**) cm
(14.5 (16.5: 18.5: 20.5: 21.5: **23: 23: 23: 23.5: 24**) in)

29 (33: 37: 41: 43: **47: 47: 47: 48: 48**) cm
(11.5 (13: 14.5: 16: 17: **18.5: 18.5: 18.5: 19: 19**) in)

WILLIAM

YARN

Rowan Rowanspun DK

	S	M	L	XL	XXL	
To fit chest	97	102	107	112	117	cm
	38	40	42	44	46	in

Two colour sweater

| A Snowball | 730 | 8 | 9 | 9 | 9 | 10 | x | 50gm |
| B Icy | 739 | 3 | 3 | 4 | 4 | 4 | x | 50gm |

One colour sweater

| | | 9 | 9 | 10 | 10 | 11 | x | 50gm |

(photographed in Goblin 736)

NEEDLES

1 pair 3¾mm (no 9) (US 5) needles
1 pair 4mm (no 8) (US 6) needles

TENSION

21 sts and 29 rows to 10 cm measured over flattened rib pattern using 4mm (US 6) needles.

Two colour sweater

BACK
Cast on 127 (133: 137: 143: 147) sts using 3¾mm (US 5) needles and yarn B.
Row 1 (RS): K1 (4: 0: 0: 1), P5 (5: 1: 4: 5), *K5, P5, rep from * to last 1 (4: 6: 9: 1) sts, K1 (4: 5: 5: 1), P0 (0: 1: 4: 0).
Row 2: P1 (4: 0: 0: 1), K5 (5: 1: 4: 5), *P5, K5, rep from * to last 1 (4: 6: 9: 1) sts, P1 (4: 5: 5: 1), K0 (0: 1: 4: 0).
These 2 rows form rib.
Work in rib for a further 8 rows, ending with a WS row.
Change to 4mm (US 6) needles.
Cont in rib until back measures 20 cm, ending with a WS row.
Break off yarn B and join in yarn A.
Using yarn A only, cont in rib until back measures 42 cm, ending with a WS row.
Shape armholes
Cast off 6 sts at beg of next 2 rows.
115 (121: 125: 131: 135) sts.
Dec 1 st at each end of next and every foll 4th row until 85 (93: 97: 105: 109) sts rem, then on foll 0 (3: 4: 7: 8) alt rows. 85 (87: 89: 91: 93) sts.
Work 1 row, ending with a WS row.
Shape shoulders
Cast off 8 (8: 9: 9: 9) sts at beg of next 4 rows, then 8 (9: 8: 9: 10) sts at beg of foll 2 rows.
Leave rem 37 sts on a holder.

FRONT
Work as given for back until 91 (97: 99: 103: 105) sts rem in armhole shaping.
Work 1 (3: 1: 1: 1) rows, ending with a WS row.
Shape neck
Next row (RS): (Work 2 tog) 0 (1: 0: 1: 1) time, rib 35 (36: 39: 39: 40) and turn, leaving rem sts on a holder. 35 (37: 39: 40: 41) sts.
Work each side of neck separately.

Dec 1 st at neck edge on next 4 rows, then on foll 3 alt rows **and at same time** dec 1 st at armhole edge on 2nd (4th: 2nd: 2nd: 2nd) and every foll 4th (alt: alt: alt: alt) row.
25 (26: 27: 28: 29) sts.
Work 1 row, ending with a WS row.
Shape shoulder
Cast off 8 (8: 9: 9: 9) sts at beg and dec 1 st at end of next row. 16 (17: 17: 18: 19) sts.
Work 1 row.
Cast off 8 (8: 9: 9: 9) sts at beg of next row.
Work 1 row. Cast off rem 8 (9: 8: 9: 10) sts.
With RS facing, slip centre 21 sts onto a holder, rejoin yarn to rem sts, rib to last 0 (2: 0: 2: 2) sts, (work 2 tog) 0 (1: 0: 1: 1) time.
Work to match first side, reversing shapings.

SLEEVES (both alike)
Cast on 69 (69: 71: 73: 73) sts using 3¾mm (US 5) needles and yarn B.
Row 1 (RS): K2 (2: 3: 4: 4), P5, *K5, P5, rep from * to last 2 (2: 3: 4: 4) sts, K2 (2: 3: 4: 4).
Row 2: P2 (2: 3: 4: 4), K5, *P5, K5, rep from * to last 2 (2: 3: 4: 4) sts, P2 (2: 3: 4: 4).
These 2 rows form rib.
Work in rib for a further 8 rows, end with a WS row.
Change to 4mm (US 6) needles.
Cont in rib, inc 1 st at each end of next and foll 10th row, taking inc sts into rib.
73 (73: 75: 77: 77) sts.
Work 9 rows, ending with a WS row.
Break off yarn B and join in yarn A.
Using yarn A only, cont in rib as folls:
Inc 1 st at each end of next and every foll 10th row to 93 (87: 89: 95: 87) sts, then on every foll 8th row until there are 95 (97: 99: 101: 103) sts.
Cont straight until sleeve measures 49 (50: 50: 51: 51) cm, ending with a WS row.
Shape top
Cast off 6 sts at beg of next 2 rows.
83 (85: 87: 89: 91) sts.
Dec 1 st at each end of next and every foll alt row until 25 sts rem.
Work 1 row, ending with a WS row.
Place markers at both ends of last row.
Dec 1 st at each end of next and every foll 6th (6th: 6th: 6th: 8th) row until 15 (17: 19: 21: 15) sts rem, then on every foll – (8th: 8th: 8th: –) row until – (15: 15: 15: –) sts rem.
Work 7 rows, ending with a WS row.
Leave rem 15 sts on a holder.

MAKING UP
PRESS all pieces as described on the info page.
Join both front and right back shoulder and armhole seams using back stitch, or mattress stitch if preferred, as folls: sew row end edges of sleeves above markers to body shoulder cast-off edges, then sew matching shaped body and sleeve edges together.
Neckband
With RS facing, 3¾mm (US 5) needles and yarn A, pick up and rib 15 sts from top of left sleeve, pick up and knit 17 sts down left side of neck, rib 21 sts from front, pick up and knit 17 sts up right side of neck, rib 15 sts from top of right sleeve, then rib across 37 sts from back as folls: P2tog, P4, (K5, P5) twice, K5, P4, P2tog. 120 sts.

Row 1 (WS): *K5, P5, rep from * to end.
Rep this row until neckband measures 18 cm.
Cast off in rib.
Join left back shoulder and armhole and neckband seam, reversing neckband seam for turn-back. See information page for finishing instructions.

One colour sweater
Work as given for two colour sweater using same colour throughout.

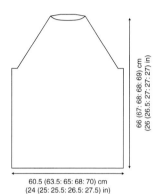

66 (67: 68: 68: 69) cm
(26 (26.5: 27: 27: 27) in)

60.5 (63.5: 65: 68: 70) cm
(24 (25: 25.5: 26.5: 27.5) in)

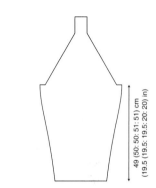

49 (50: 50: 51: 51) cm
(19.5 (19.5: 19.5: 20: 20) in)

William Sweater knitted in Rowanspun DK, Heather Cardigan knitted in Kid Classic, knitting instructions on page 14 & Fin Beret knitted in Kidsilk Haze, knitting instructions on page 77

William Sweater knitted in Rowanspun DK, knitting instructions on page 41, Heather Cardigan knitted in Kid Classic, knitting instructions on page 14 & Fin Beret knitted in Kidsilk Haze, knitting instructions on page 77

DUNOON

YARN

Rowan Rowanspun DK, Kid Classic and Kidsilk Haze

	XS	S	M	L	XL		
To fit bust	81	86	91	97	102		cm
	32	34	36	38	40		in
Rowanspun DK							
A Chilli 732	3	3	4	4	4	x	50gm
B Eau de nil 735	2	3	3	3	3	x	50gm
Kid Classic							
C Swirl 834	1	1	1	1	1	x	50gm
Kidsilk Haze★							
D Wicked 599	1	1	1	1	1	x	25gm
E Poison 594	1	1	1	1	1	x	25gm
F Lord 593	1	1	1	1	1	x	25gm

★ Use Kidsilk Haze **DOUBLE** throughout.

NEEDLES

1 pair 3¼mm (no 10) (US 3) needles
1 pair 3¾mm (no 9) (US 5) needles
1 pair 4mm (no 8) (US 6) needles

BUTTONS - 8

TENSION

21 sts and 29 rows to 10 cm measured over patterned stocking stitch using 4mm (US 6) needles.

BACK

Cast on 85 (91: 97: 103: 109) sts using 3¾mm (US 5) needles and yarn A.
Using the **intarsia** technique as described on the information page, starting and ending rows as indicated and repeating the 30 row repeat throughout, cont in patt foll chart, which is worked entirely in st st, as folls:
Work 6 rows.
Change to 4mm (US 6) needles.
Work 8 rows.
Inc 1 st at each end of next and every foll 14th row until there are 95 (101: 107: 113: 119) sts, taking inc sts into patt.
Cont straight until back measures 27 (28: 28: 29: 29) cm, ending with a WS row.

Shape armholes

Keeping patt correct, cast off 3 (4: 4: 5: 5) sts at beg of next 2 rows. 89 (93: 99: 103: 109) sts.
Dec 1 st at each end of next 5 (5: 7: 7: 9) rows, then on foll 3 (4: 4: 5: 5) alt rows. 73 (75: 77: 79: 81) sts.
Cont straight until armhole measures 20 (20: 21: 21: 22) cm, ending with a WS row.

Shape shoulders and back neck

Keeping patt correct, cast off 7 sts at beg of next 2 rows. 59 (61: 63: 65: 67) sts.
Next row (RS): Cast off 7 sts, patt until there are 10 (10: 11: 11: 12) sts on right needle and turn, leaving rem sts on a holder.
Work each side of neck separately.
Cast off 4 sts at beg of next row.
Cast off rem 6 (6: 7: 7: 8) sts.
With RS facing, rejoin yarn to rem sts, cast off centre 25 (27: 27: 29: 29) sts, patt to end.
Work to match first side, reversing shapings.

LEFT FRONT

Cast on 45 (48: 51: 54: 57) sts using 3¾mm (US 5) needles and yarn A.
Cont in patt foll chart as folls:
Work 6 rows.
Change to 4mm (US 6) needles.
Work 8 rows.
Inc 1 st at beg of next and every foll 14th row until there are 50 (53: 56: 59: 62) sts, taking inc sts into patt.
Cont straight until left front matches back to beg of armhole shaping, ending with a WS row.

Shape armhole

Keeping patt correct, cast off 3 (4: 4: 5: 5) sts at beg of next row. 47 (49: 52: 54: 57) sts.
Work 1 row.
Dec 1 st at armhole edge of next 5 (5: 7: 7: 9) rows, then on foll 3 (4: 4: 5: 5) alt rows.
39 (40: 41: 42: 43) sts.
Cont straight until 19 (19: 19: 21: 21) rows less have been worked than on back to start of shoulder shaping, ending with a RS row.

Shape neck

Keeping patt correct, cast off 11 (12: 12: 12: 12) sts at beg of next row. 28 (28: 29: 30: 31) sts.
Dec 1 st at neck edge on next 5 rows, then on foll 2 (2: 2: 3: 3) alt rows, then on foll 4th row.
20 (20: 21: 21: 22) sts.
Work 5 rows, ending with a WS row.

Shape shoulder

Keeping patt correct, cast off 7 sts at beg of next and foll alt row.
Work 1 row. Cast off rem 6 (6: 7: 7: 8) sts.

RIGHT FRONT

Cast on 45 (48: 51: 54: 57) sts using 3¾mm (US 5) needles and yarn A.
Cont in patt foll chart as folls: Work 6 rows.
Change to 4mm (US 6) needles.
Work 8 rows.
Inc 1 st at end of next and every foll 14th row until there are 50 (53: 56: 59: 62) sts, taking inc sts into patt.
Complete to match left front, reversing shapings.

(Knitting instructions continued on page 87)

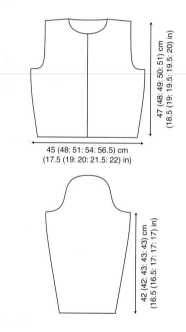

47 (48: 49: 50: 51) cm
(18.5 (19: 19.5: 19.5: 20) in)

45 (48: 51: 54: 56.5) cm
(17.5 (19: 20: 21.5: 22) in)

42 (42: 43: 43: 43) cm
(16.5 (16.5: 17: 17: 17) in)

Key ■ A ■ B ■ C ■ D ■ E ■ F

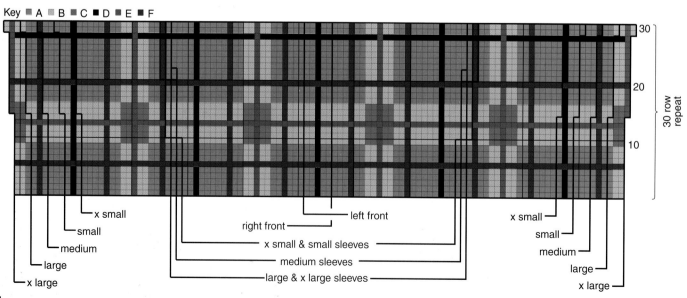

30
20
10
30 row repeat

x small
small
medium
large
x large

right front
left front
x small & small sleeves
medium sleeves
large & x large sleeves

x small
small
medium
large
x large

DENNY

YARN
Rowan Rowanspun 4 ply

	XS	S	M	L	XL	
To fit bust	81	86	91	97	102 cm	
	32	34	36	38	40 in	
A Stone	702	6	7	7	8	8 x 25gm
B Slate	704	6	7	7	8	8 x 25gm

NEEDLES
1 pair 2¾mm (no 12) (US 2) needles
1 pair 3¼mm (no 10) (US 3) needles

BUTTONS - 7

TENSION
31 sts and 32 rows to 10 cm measured over patterned stocking stitch using 3¼mm (US 3) needles.

BACK
Cast on 117 (125: 133: 139: 147) sts using 2¾mm (US 2) needles and yarn A.
Row 1 (RS): K1, *P1, K1, rep from * to end.
Row 2: As row 1.
These 2 rows form moss st.
Work in moss st for a further 3 rows, ending with a RS row.
Join in yarn B.
Row 6 (WS): Using yarn B P1, *using yarn A P1, using yarn B P1, rep from * to end.
Break off yarn B.
Work in moss st for 5 rows.
Row 12 (WS) (inc): P2 (6: 3: 5: 1), *M1, P8 (8: 9: 8: 9), rep from * to last 3 (7: 4: 6: 2) sts, M1, P3 (7: 4: 6: 2). 132 (140: 148: 156: 164) sts.
Change to 3¼mm (US 3) needles.
Join in yarn B.
Using the **fairisle** technique as described on the information page, repeating the 4 st pattern repeat 33 (35: 37: 39: 41) times across rows and repeating the 4 row repeat throughout, cont in patt foll chart, which is worked entirely in st st, as folls:
Work 4 rows.
Dec 1 st at each end of next and every foll 4th row until 118 (126: 134: 142: 150) sts rem.
Work 5 (7: 7: 9: 9) rows.

Inc 1 st at each end of next and every foll 6th row to 132 (140: 148: 156: 164) sts, then on every foll 4th row until there are 140 (148: 156: 164: 172) sts, taking inc sts into patt.
Cont straight until back measures 34 (35: 35: 36: 36) cm, ending with a WS row.
Shape armholes
Keeping patt correct, cast off 5 (6: 6: 7: 7) sts at beg of next 2 rows. 130 (136: 144: 150: 158) sts.
Dec 1 st at each end of next 9 (9: 11: 11: 13) rows, then on foll 4 (5: 5: 6: 6) alt rows.
104 (108: 112: 116: 120) sts.
Cont straight until armhole measures 20 (20: 21: 21: 22) cm, ending with a WS row.
Shape shoulders and back neck
Keeping patt correct, cast off 10 (11: 11: 12: 12) sts at beg of next 2 rows.
84 (86: 90: 92: 96) sts.
Next row (RS): Cast off 10 (11: 11: 12: 12) sts, patt until there are 15 (14: 16: 15: 17) sts on right needle and turn, leaving rem sts on a holder.
Work each side of neck separately.
Cast off 4 sts at beg of next row.
Cast off rem 11 (10: 12: 11: 13) sts.
With RS facing, rejoin yarn to rem sts, cast off centre 34 (36: 36: 38: 38) sts, patt to end.
Work to match first side, reversing shapings.

LEFT FRONT
Cast on 67 (71: 75: 79: 83) sts using 2¾mm (US 2) needles and yarn A.
Work in moss st as given for back for 5 rows, ending with a RS row.
Join in yarn B.
Row 6 (WS): Using yarn A (K1, P1) twice, using yarn B P1, *using yarn A P1, using yarn B P1, rep from * to end.
Break off yarn B.
Work in moss st for a further 5 rows.
Row 12 (WS) (inc): Moss st 9 sts and slip these 9 sts onto a holder for border, P5 (4: 6: 5: 7), *M1, P8 (9: 9: 10: 10), rep from * to last 5 (4: 6: 5: 7) sts, M1, P5 (4: 6: 5: 7). 65 (69: 73: 77: 81) sts.
Change to 3¼mm (US 3) needles.
Join in yarn B.
Starting and ending rows as indicated, repeating the 4 st pattern repeat 16 (17: 18: 19: 20) times across rows and repeating the 4 row repeat throughout, cont in patt foll chart as folls:
Work 4 rows.
Dec 1 st at beg of next and every foll 4th row until 58 (62: 66: 70: 74) sts rem.
Work 5 (7: 7: 9: 9) rows.
Inc 1 st at beg of next and every foll 6th row to 65 (69: 73: 77: 81) sts, then on every foll 4th row until there are 69 (73: 77: 81: 85) sts, taking inc sts into patt.
Cont straight until left front matches back to beg of armhole shaping, ending with a WS row.
Shape armhole
Keeping patt correct, cast off 5 (6: 6: 7: 7) sts at beg of next row. 64 (67: 71: 74: 78) sts.
Work 1 row.
Dec 1 st at armhole edge of next 9 (9: 11: 11: 13) rows, then on foll 4 (5: 5: 6: 6) alt rows.
51 (53: 55: 57: 59) sts.
Cont straight until 21 (21: 21: 23: 23) rows less have been worked than on back to start of shoulder shaping, ending with a RS row.

Shape neck
Keeping patt correct, cast off 9 (10: 10: 10: 10) sts at beg of next row, then 4 sts at beg of foll alt row. 38 (39: 41: 43: 45) sts.
Dec 1 st at neck edge on next 3 rows, then on foll 3 (3: 3: 4: 4) alt rows, then on foll 4th row. 31 (32: 34: 35: 37) sts.
Work 5 rows, ending with a WS row.
Shape shoulder
Keeping patt correct, cast off 10 (11: 11: 12: 12) sts at beg of next and foll alt row.
Work 1 row.
Cast off rem 11 (10: 12: 11: 13) sts.

RIGHT FRONT
Cast on 67 (71: 75: 79: 83) sts using 2¾mm (US 2) needles and yarn A.
Work in moss st as given for back for 5 rows, ending with a RS row.
Join in yarn B.
Row 6 (WS): *Using yarn B P1, using yarn A P1, rep from * to last 5 sts, using yarn B P1, using yarn A (P1, K1) twice.
Break off yarn B.
Work in moss st for a further 5 rows.
Row 12 (WS) (inc): P5 (4: 6: 5: 7), *M1, P8 (9: 9: 10: 10), rep from * to last 14 (13: 15: 14: 16) sts, M1, P5 (4: 6: 5: 7) and turn, leaving last 9 sts on a holder for border. 65 (69: 73: 77: 81) sts.
Change to 3¼mm (US 3) needles.
Join in yarn B.
Starting and ending rows as indicated, repeating the 4 st pattern repeat 16 (17: 18: 19: 20) times across rows and repeating the 4 row repeat throughout, cont in patt foll chart as folls:
Work 4 rows.
Dec 1 st at end of next and every foll 4th row until 58 (62: 66: 70: 74) sts rem.
Complete to match left front, reversing shapings.

(Knitting instructions continued on page 87)

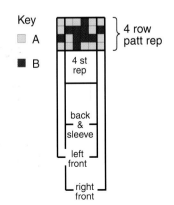

Key
A
B
4 row patt rep
4 st rep
back & sleeve
left front
right front

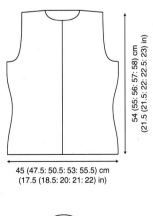

54 (55: 56: 57: 58) cm
(21.5 (21.5: 22: 22.5: 23) in)

45 (47.5: 50.5: 53: 55.5) cm
(17.5 (18.5: 20: 21: 22) in)

42 (42: 43: 43: 43) cm
(16.5 (16.5: 17: 17: 17) in)

SPENCER

YARN

Rowan Rowanspun DK and Kid Classic

		ladies			mens		
		S	M	L	M	L	XL	
To fit bust/chest		86	91	97	102	107	112	cm
					34	36	38	40	42	44	in

Rowan Rowanspun DK

A Chilli	732	5	6	6	7	7	8	x 50gm
B Punch	731	2	2	2	2	3	3	x 50gm

Rowan Rowanspun DK and Kid Classic
Rowanspun DK

A Icy	739	6	6	7	8	8	9	x 50gm
Kid Classic								
B Smoke	831	2	2	2	2	3	3	x 50gm

NEEDLES

1 pair 3¼mm (no 10) (US 3) needles
1 pair 4mm (no 8) (US 6) needles

TENSION

24 sts and 28 rows to 10 cm measured over front pattern, 21 sts and 29 rows to 10 cm measured over flattened rib pattern using 4mm (US 6) needles.

Pattern note: The pattern is written for the 3 ladies sizes, followed by the 3 mens sizes in **bold**. Where only one figure appears this applies to all sizes in that group.

BACK

Cast on 83 (89: 95: **101: 107: 113**) sts using 3¼mm (US 3) needles and yarn A.
Row 1 (RS): K1, *P3, K3, rep from * to last 4 sts, P3, K1.
Row 2: P1, *K3, P3, rep from * to last 4 sts, K3, P1.
These 2 rows form rib.
Work in rib for a further 14 rows.
Change to 4mm (US 6) needles.
Cont in rib, shaping sides by inc 1 st at each end of 3rd and every foll 10th (**14th**) row to 89 (95: 101: **107: 113: 119**) sts, then on every foll 8th (**10th**) row until there are 99 (105: 111: **117: 123: 129**) sts, taking inc sts into rib. Cont straight until back measures 31 (**39**) cm, ending with a WS row.
Shape armholes
Cast off 4 (5: 5: **5: 5: 6**) sts at beg of next 2 rows.
91 (95: 101: **107: 113: 117**) sts.
Dec 1 st at each end of next 5 (5: 7: **5: 7: 7**) rows, then on foll 4 (5: 5: **5: 5: 6**) alt rows.
73 (75: 77: **87: 89: 91**) sts.
Cont straight until armhole measures 20 (21: 22: **23: 24: 25**) cm, ending with a WS row.
Shape shoulders and back neck
Cast off 7 (**8**) sts at beg of next 2 rows.
59 (61: 63: **71: 73: 75**) sts.

Next row (RS): Cast off 7 (**8**) sts, rib until there are 10 (11: 11: **12: 13: 13**) sts on right needle and turn, leaving rem sts on a holder.
Work each side of neck separately.
Cast off 4 sts at beg of next row.
Cast off rem 6 (7: 7: **8: 9: 9**) sts.
With RS facing, rejoin yarn to rem sts, cast off centre 25 (25: 27: **31: 31: 33**) sts, rib to end.
Work to match first side, reversing shapings.

FRONT

Cast on 83 (89: 95: **101: 107: 113**) sts using 3¼mm (US 3) needles and yarn A.
Work in rib as given for back for 15 rows, ending with a RS row.
Row 16 (WS) (inc): Rib 3 (6: 3: **5: 1: 4**), *M1, rib 7 (7: 8: **6: 7: 7**), rep from * to last 3 (6: 4: **6: 1: 4**) sts, M1, rib 3 (6: 4: **6: 1: 4**).
95 (101: 107: **117: 123: 129**) sts.
Change to 4mm (US 6) needles.
Using the **fairisle** technique as described on the information page, starting and ending rows as indicated, working chart rows 1 and 2 once only and then repeating the 14 row repeat throughout, cont in patt foll chart, which is worked entirely in st st, as folls:
Inc 1 st at each end of 3rd and every foll 8th (**10th**) row to 101 (107: 113: **131: 137: 143**) sts, then on every foll 6th (**8th**) row until there are 115 (121: 127: **135: 141: 147**) sts, taking inc sts into patt.
Cont straight until front meas same as back to beg of armhole shaping, ending with a WS row.
Shape armholes
Keeping patt correct, cast off 5 (6: 6: **5: 6: 6**) sts at beg of next 2 rows. 105 (109: 115: **125: 129: 135**) sts.
Dec 1 st at each end of next 5 (5: 7: **7: 7: 9**) rows, then on foll 5 (6: 6: **5: 6: 6**) alt rows.
85 (87: 89: **101: 103: 105**) sts.
Cont straight until armhole measures 14 (15: 16: **16: 17: 18**) cm, ending with a WS row.
Shape neck
Next row (RS): Patt 34 (35: 35: **40: 41: 41**) sts and turn, leaving rem sts on a holder.
Work each side of neck separately. Cast off 4 (**5**) sts at beg of next row. 30 (31: 31: **35: 36: 36**) sts.
Dec 1 st at neck edge of next 3 rows, then on foll 2 alt rows, then on foll 4th row.
24 (25: 25: **29: 30: 30**) sts.
Cont straight until front meas same as back to start of shoulder shaping, ending with a WS row.
Shape shoulder
Cast off 8 (**10**) sts at beg of next and foll alt row.
Work 1 row. Cast off rem 8 (9: 9: **9: 10: 10**) sts.
With RS facing, rejoin yarn to rem sts, cast off centre 17 (17: 19: **21: 21: 23**) sts, patt to end.
Work to match first side, reversing shapings.

SLEEVES (both alike)

Cast on 49 (51: 53: **59: 61: 63**) sts using 3¼mm (US 3) needles and yarn A.
Row 1 (RS): K2 (3: 1: **1: 2: 3**), *P3, K3, rep from * to last 5 (6: 4: **4: 5: 6**) sts, P3, K2 (3: 1: **1: 2: 3**).
Row 2: P2 (3: 1: **1: 2: 3**), *K3, P3, rep from * to last 5 (6: 4: **4: 5: 6**) sts, K3, P2 (3: 1: **1: 2: 3**).
These 2 rows form rib.
Work in rib for a further 8 rows.
Change to 4mm (US 6) needles.
Cont in rib, shaping sides by inc 1 st at each end of 7th and every foll 10th row to 71 (67: 65: **85: 81: 79**) sts, then on every foll – (8th: 8th: **–: 8th: 8th**) row until there are – (75: 79: **–: 89: 93**) sts, taking inc sts into rib.
Cont straight until sleeve measures 43 (44: 45: **50: 51: 52**) cm, ending with a WS row.
Shape top
Cast off 4 (5: 5: **5: 5: 6**) sts at beg of next 2 rows.
63 (65: 69: **75: 79: 81**) sts.
Dec 1 st at each end of next 3 rows, then on foll 2 (**3**) alt rows, then on every foll 4th row until 43 (45: 51: **51: 57: 59**) sts rem.
Work 1 row, ending with a WS row.
Dec 1 st at each end of next and foll 3 (4: 7: **3: 6: 7**) alt rows, then on foll 3 rows.
Cast off rem 29 (**37**) sts.

(Knitting instructions continued on page 87)

47 (48: 49: 50: 51) cm
(18.5: 19: 19.5: 19.5: 20) in

48 (50.5: 53: **56: 59: 61.5**) cm
(19 (20: 21: **22: 23: 24**) in)

43 (44: 45: **50: 51: 52**) cm
(17 (17.5: 17.5: **19.5: 20: 20.5**) in)

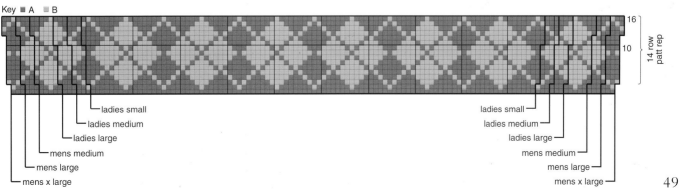

Key ■ A ■ B

16

10

14 row patt rep

ladies small
ladies medium
ladies large
mens medium
mens large
mens x large

ladies small
ladies medium
ladies large
mens medium
mens large
mens x large

JOHNSTONE GLOVES

YARN
Rowan Kidsilk Haze and Rowanspun DK
To fit average sized adult hand
Frilled gloves

A	Kidsilk Haze★	Liqueur	595	1	x 25gm
B	Rowanspun DK	Chilli	732	2	x 50gm

Narrow striped gloves

A	Kidsilk Haze★	Liqueur	595	1	x 25gm
B	Kidsilk Haze★	Marmalade	596	1	x 25gm

Wider striped gloves

A	Rowanspun DK	Lavender	733	1	x 50gm
B	Rowanspun DK	Punch	731	1	x 50gm

★ Use Kidsilk Haze **DOUBLE** throughout.

NEEDLES
1 pair 3mm (no 11) (US 2/3) needles
1 pair 3¼mm (no 10) (US 3) needles

TENSION
26 sts and 36 rows to 10 cm measured over stocking stitch using 3¼mm (US 3) needles.

Frilled Gloves
Cast on 181 sts using 3mm (US 2/3) needles and yarn A.
Break off yarn A and join in yarn B.
Row 1 (RS): K1, ★K2, lift first of these 2 sts over 2nd st and off right needle, rep from ★ to end. 91 sts.
Row 2: P1, ★P2tog, rep from ★ to end. 46 sts.
Cast on 46 sts using 3mm (US 2/3) needles.
★★Row 1 (RS): K2, ★P2, K2, rep from ★ to end.
Row 2: P2, ★K2, P2, rep from ★ to end.
These 2 rows form rib.
Work in rib for a further 28 rows, dec 1 st at end of last row. 45 sts.
Change to 3¼mm (US 3) needles.
Beg with a K row, cont in st st as folls:
Work 14 rows, ending with a WS row.

Shape thumb gusset
Row 1 (RS): K21, M1, K3, M1, K21. 47 sts.
Row 2 and every foll alt row: Purl.
Row 3: K21, M1, K5, M1, K21. 49 sts.
Row 5: K21, M1, K7, M1, K21. 51 sts.
Row 7: K21, M1, K9, M1, K21. 53 sts.
Row 8: Purl.
Divide for thumb
Next row (RS): K32 and turn.
Next row: P11 and turn.
Working on these sts only for thumb, cont as folls:
Cast on 3 sts at beg of next row. 14 sts.
Work a further 17 rows, ending with a WS row.
Break yarn and thread through all 14 sts.
Pull up tight and fasten off securely.
Sew thumb seam.
With RS facing, rejoin yarn to rem sts and pick up and K 3 sts from base of thumb, K rem 21 sts. 45 sts.
Work 11 rows, ending with a WS row.
Work first finger
Next row (RS): K29 and turn.
Next row: Cast on and P one st, P13 and turn.
Working on these sts only for first finger, cont as folls:
Cast on 1 st at beg of next row. 15 sts.
Work a further 23 rows, ending with a WS row.
Break yarn and thread through all 15 sts. Pull up tight and fasten off securely. Sew seam.
Work second finger
With RS facing, rejoin yarn to rem sts and pick up and K 2 sts from base of first finger, K6 and turn.
Next row (WS): Cast on and P one st, P14 and turn.
Working on these sts only for second finger, cont as folls:
Cast on 1 st at beg of next row. 16 sts.
Work a further 25 rows, ending with a WS row.
Break yarn and thread through all 16 sts. Pull up tight and fasten off securely. Sew seam.

Work third finger
With RS facing, rejoin yarn to rem sts and pick up and K 2 sts from base of second finger, K5 and turn.
Next row (WS): Cast on and P one st, P12 and turn.
Working on these sts only for third finger, cont as folls:
Cast on 1 st at beg of next row. 14 sts.
Work a further 21 rows, ending with a WS row.
Break yarn and thread through all 14 sts. Pull up tight and fasten off securely. Sew seam.
Work fourth finger
With RS facing, rejoin yarn to rem sts and pick up and K 2 sts from base of third finger, K to end.
Working on these 12 sts only for fourth finger, cont as folls:
Work a further 17 rows, ending with a WS row.
Break yarn and thread through all 12 sts. Pull up tight and fasten off securely. Sew side and finger seam. Make a second glove in exactly the same way.

Narrow Striped Gloves
Cast on 46 sts using 3mm (US 2/3) needles and yarn A.
Work as given for frilled gloves from ★★ until all 30 rows of rib have been worked.
Join in yarn B.
Working in 4 row stripe sequence of 2 rows using yarn A and 2 rows using yarn B, complete as given for frilled gloves.

Wider Striped Gloves
Cast on 46 sts using 3mm (US 2/3) needles and yarn A.
Work as given for frilled gloves from ★★ until all 30 rows of rib and first 2 rows of st st have been worked.
Join in yarn B.
Working in 8 row stripe sequence of 4 rows using yarn B and 4 rows using yarn A, complete as given for frilled gloves.

LORNA SCARF

YARN
Rowan Kid Classic and Kidsilk Haze

A	Kid Classic★	Juicy	827	3	x 50gm
B	Kidsilk Haze	Marmalade	596	1	x 25gm

★Use **DOUBLE** throughout.

NEEDLES
1 pair 9mm (no 00) (US 13) needles

TENSION
11 sts and 16 rows to 10 cm measured over moss stitch using 9mm (US 13) needles.

FINISHED SIZE
Completed scarf is approx 22 cm (8½ in) by 154 cm (60½ in), including fringe.

Scarf
Using 9mm (US 13) needles cast on 25 sts using **two strands of yarn A** held together.
Row 1 (RS): K1, ★P1, K1, rep from ★ to end.
Row 2: As row 1.
These 2 rows form moss st.
Cont in moss st until scarf measures 130 cm.
Cast off in moss st.

MAKING UP
PRESS as described on the information page.
Cut 27 cm lengths of yarn B and knot groups of 4 of these lengths of yarn through each st across both ends of scarf to form fringe.

Johnstone Gloves knitted in Kidsilk Haze, Lorna Scarf knitted in Kid Classic & Kidsilk Haze

BERRY

YARN

Rowan Rowanspun 4 ply and Kidsilk Haze

	XS	S	M	L	XL		
To fit bust	81	86	91	97	102	cm	
	32	34	36	38	40	in	
Kidsilk Haze★							
A Wicked 599	2	2	2	2	2	x	25gm
Rowanspun 4 ply							
B Slate 704	4	5	5	5	6	x	25gm

★ Use **DOUBLE** throughout.

NEEDLES

1 pair 2¼mm (no 13) (US 1) needles
1 pair 3mm (no 11) (US 2/3) needles

BUTTONS – 48 (52: 56: 60: 64) for optional trim

TENSION

28 sts and 40 rows to 10 cm measured over stocking stitch using 3mm (US 2/3) needles and yarn B.

BACK

Cast on 98 (106: 114: 122: 130) sts using 2¼mm (US 1) needles and yarn A.
Row 1 (RS): K2, *P2, K2, rep from * to end.
Row 2: P2, *K2, P2, rep from * to end.
These 2 rows form rib.
Work in rib for a further 32 rows, inc 1 st at centre of last row and ending with a WS row.
99 (107: 115: 123: 131) sts.
Break off yarn A and join in yarn B.
Change to 3mm (US 2/3) needles.
Beg with a K row, cont in st st, as folls:
Work 10 rows.
Next row (RS) (inc): K3, M1, K to last 3 sts, M1, K3.
Working all increases 3 sts in from ends of rows as set by last row, inc 1 st at each end of every foll 10th row until there are 113 (121: 129: 137: 145) sts.
Cont straight until back measures 28 (29: 29: 30: 30) cm, ending with a WS row.
Shape armholes
Cast off 4 (4: 4: 6: 6) sts at beg of next 2 rows.
105 (113: 121: 125: 133) sts.
Next row (RS) (dec): K3, K3tog, K to last 6 sts, K3tog tbl, K3.
Working all decreases as set by last row, cont as folls:
Work 1 row.
Dec 2 sts at each end of next and foll 0 (1: 2: 2: 3) alt rows, then on every foll 4th row until 89 (93: 97: 101: 105) sts rem.
Cont straight until armhole measures 20 (20: 21: 21: 22) cm, ending with a WS row.
Shape shoulders and back neck
Cast off 8 (8: 9: 9: 10) sts at beg of next 2 rows.
73 (77: 79: 83: 85) sts.
Next row (RS): Cast off 8 (8: 9: 9: 10) sts, K until there are 11 (12: 12: 13: 13) sts on right needle and turn, leaving rem sts on a holder.
Work each side of neck separately.
Cast off 4 sts at beg of next row.
Cast off rem 7 (8: 8: 9: 9) sts.
With RS facing, rejoin yarn to rem sts, cast off centre 35 (37: 37: 39: 39) sts, K to end.
Work to match first side, reversing shapings.

FRONT

Work as given for back until 30 (30: 30: 32: 32) rows less have been worked than on back to start of shoulder shaping, ending with a WS row.
Shape neck
Next row (RS): K35 (36: 38: 40: 42) and turn, leaving rem sts on a holder.
Work each side of neck separately.
Cast off 4 sts at beg of next row.
31 (32: 34: 36: 38) sts.
Dec 1 st at neck edge of next 3 rows, then on foll 2 (2: 2: 3: 3) alt rows, then on every foll 4th row until 23 (24: 26: 27: 29) sts rem.
Work 9 rows, ending with a WS row.
Shape shoulder
Cast off 8 (8: 9: 9: 10) sts at beg of next and foll alt row.
Work 1 row. Cast off rem 7 (8: 8: 9: 9) sts.
With RS facing, rejoin yarn to rem sts, cast off centre 19 (21: 21: 21: 21) sts, K to end.
Work to match first side, reversing shapings.

SLEEVES (both alike)
Cast on 86 (90: 90: 94: 94) sts using 2¼mm (US 1) needles and yarn B.
Work in rib as given for back for 6 rows, inc (dec: inc: dec: inc) 1 st at centre of last row.
87 (89: 91: 93: 95) sts.
Change to 3mm (US 2/3) needles.
Beg with a K row, cont in st st, as folls:
Work 10 rows, inc 1 st at each end of 3rd of these rows. 89 (91: 93: 95: 97) sts.

Shape top

Cast off 4 (4: 4: 6: 6) sts at beg of next 2 rows.
81 (83: 85: 83: 85) sts.
Dec 1 st at each end of next 5 rows, then on foll 3 alt rows, then on every foll 4th row until 49 (51: 53: 47: 49) sts rem.
Work 1 row, ending with a WS row.
Dec 1 st at each end of next and foll 1 (2: 3: 0: 1) alt rows, then on foll 3 rows.
39 sts.
Cast off 4 sts at beg of next 2 rows.
Cast off rem 31 sts.

MAKING UP

PRESS all pieces as described on the info page.
Join right shoulder seam using back stitch, or mattress stitch if preferred.
Neckband
With RS facing, 2¼mm (US 1) and yarn B, pick up and knit 34 (36: 36: 39: 39) sts down left side of neck, 19 (21: 21: 21: 21) sts from front, 34 (36: 36: 39: 39) sts up right side of neck, then 43 (45: 45: 47: 47) sts from back.
130 (138: 138: 146: 146) sts.
Beg with a WS row, work in rib as given for back for 6 rows.
Cast off in rib (on WS).
See information page for finishing instructions, setting in sleeves using the set-in method.
If desired, sew buttons in place around body, positioning each button 1 cm above each pair of P sts of rib.

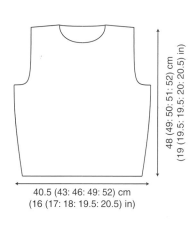

40.5 (43: 46: 49: 52) cm
(16 (17: 18: 19.5: 20.5) in)

48 (49: 50: 51: 52) cm
(19 (19.5: 19.5: 20: 20.5) in)

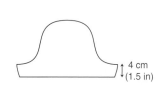

4 cm
(1.5 in)

ISLA

YARN

Rowan Rowanspun 4 ply and Lurex Shimmer

		XS	S	M	L	XL		
To fit bust		81	86	91	97	102	cm	
		32	34	36	38	40	in	

Cardigan

Lurex Shimmer

A Copper	330	1	1	1	1	1	x	25gm
B Bronze	335	2	2	2	3	3	x	25gm

Rowanspun 4 ply

C Rumtoft	703	9	9	10	10	10	x	25gm

Sweater

Lurex Shimmer

A Claret	331	1	1	1	1	1	x	25gm

Rowanspun 4 ply

B Burgundy	710	8	8	8	9	9	x	25gm

NEEDLES

1 pair 2¼mm (no 13) (US 1) needles
1 pair 3mm (no 11) (US 2/3) needles

BUTTONS – 13 for cardigan

TENSION

28 sts and 40 rows to 10 cm measured over stocking stitch using 3mm (US 2/3) needles and Rowanspun 4 ply.

Cardigan

BACK

Cast on 113 (121: 129: 137: 145) sts using 2¼mm (US 1) needles and yarn A.
Row 1 (RS): P0 (2: 0: 0: 2), K1 (3: 3: 1: 3), *P3, K3, rep from * to last 4 (2: 0: 4: 2) sts, P3 (2: 0: 3: 2), K1 (0: 0: 1: 0).
Row 2: K0 (2: 0: 0: 2), P1 (3: 3: 1: 3), *K3, P3, rep from * to last 4 (2: 0: 4: 2) sts, K3 (2: 0: 3: 2), P1 (0: 0: 1: 0).
These 2 rows form rib.
Work in rib for a further 2 rows, ending with a WS row.
Break off yarn A and join in yarn B.
Cont in rib, dec 1 st at each end of 11th and foll 6th row. 109 (117: 125: 133: 141) sts.
Work a further 5 rows, ending with a WS row. (26 rows of rib completed.)
Break off yarn B and join in yarn C.
Change to 3mm (US 2/3) needles.
Beg with a K row, cont in st st, as folls:
Dec 1 st at each end of next and every foll 6th row until 99 (107: 115: 123: 131) sts rem.
Work 9 rows, ending with a WS row.
Inc 1 st at each end of next and every foll 8th row to 111 (119: 127: 135: 143) sts, then on every foll 6th row until there are 119 (127: 135: 143: 151) sts.
Cont straight until back measures 34 cm, ending with a WS row.
Shape raglan armholes
Cast off 8 sts at beg of next 2 rows.
103 (111: 119: 127: 135) sts.**
Extra small size only
Dec 1 st at each end of next and foll 4th row. 99 sts.
Work 3 rows.
All sizes
Dec 1 st at each end of next 1 (1: 7: 11: 17) rows, then on every foll alt row until 31 (33: 33: 35: 35) sts rem.
Work 1 row, ending with a WS row.
Cast off.

LEFT FRONT

Cast on 56 (60: 64: 68: 72) sts using 2¼mm (US 1) needles and yarn A.
Row 1 (RS): P0 (2: 0: 0: 2), K1 (3: 3: 1: 3), *P3, K3, rep from * to last st, P1.
Row 2: K1, P3, *K3, P3, rep from * to last 4 (2: 0: 4: 2) sts, K3 (2: 0: 3: 2), P1 (0: 0: 1: 0).
These 2 rows form rib.
Work in rib for a further 2 rows, end with a WS row.
Break off yarn A and join in yarn B.
Cont in rib, dec 1 st at beg of 11th and foll 6th row. 54 (58: 62: 66: 70) sts.
Work a further 5 rows, ending with a WS row. (26 rows of rib completed.)
Break off yarn B and join in yarn C.
Change to 3mm (US 2/3) needles.
Beg with a K row, cont in st st, as folls:
Dec 1 st at beg of next and every foll 6th row until 49 (53: 57: 61: 65) sts rem.
Work 9 rows, ending with a WS row.
Inc 1 st at beg of next and every foll 8th row to 55 (59: 63: 67: 71) sts, then on every foll 6th row until there are 59 (63: 67: 71: 75) sts.
Cont straight until left front matches back to beg of raglan armhole shaping, ending with a WS row.
Shape raglan armhole
Cast off 8 sts at beg of next row. 51 (55: 59: 63: 67) sts.
Work 1 row.**
Extra small size only
Dec 1 st at raglan edge of next and foll 4th row. 49 sts.
Work 3 rows.
All sizes
Dec 1 st at raglan edge of next 1 (1: 7: 11: 17) rows, then on every foll alt row until 23 (24: 24: 26: 26) sts rem, ending with a RS row.
Shape neck
Cast off 7 (8: 8: 8: 8) sts at beg of next row.
16 (16: 16: 18: 18) sts.
Dec 1 st at neck edge of next 5 rows, then on foll 3 (3: 3: 4: 4) alt rows **and at same time** dec 1 st at raglan edge on next and every foll alt row. 2 sts.
Work 1 row.
Next row (RS): K2tog and fasten off.

RIGHT FRONT

Cast on 56 (60: 64: 68: 72) sts using 2¼mm (US 1) needles and yarn A.
Row 1 (RS): P1, K3, *P3, K3, rep from * to last 4 (2: 0: 4: 2) sts, P3 (2: 0: 3: 2), K1 (0: 0: 1: 0).
Row 2: K0 (2: 0: 0: 2), P1 (3: 3: 1: 3), *K3, P3, rep from * to last st, K1.
These 2 rows form rib.
Work in rib for a further 2 rows, end with a WS row.
Break off yarn A and join in yarn B.
Cont in rib, dec 1 st at end of 11th and foll 6th row. 54 (58: 62: 66: 70) sts.
Complete to match left front, reversing shapings.

SLEEVES

Cast on 67 (67: 69: 71: 71) sts using 2¼mm (US 1) needles and yarn A.
Row 1 (RS): P2 (2: 3: 0: 0), K3 (3: 3: 1: 1), *P3, K3, rep from * to last 2 (2: 3: 4: 4) sts, P2 (2: 3: 3: 3), K0 (0: 0: 1: 1).
Row 2: K2 (2: 3: 0: 0), P3 (3: 3: 1: 1), *K3, P3, rep from * to last 2 (2: 3: 4: 4) sts, K2 (2: 3: 3: 3), P0 (0: 0: 1: 1).
These 2 rows form rib.
Work in rib for a further 2 rows, end with a WS row.

Break off yarn A and join in yarn B.
Cont in rib, inc 1 st at each end of 7th and foll 10th row. 71 (71: 73: 75: 75) sts.
Work a further 5 rows, ending with a WS row. (26 rows of rib completed.)
Break off yarn B and join in yarn C.
Change to 3mm (US 2/3) needles.
Beg with a K row, cont in st st, as folls:
Inc 1 st at each end of 5th and every foll 10th row to 91 (83: 85: 91: 83) sts, then on every foll 8th row until there are 101 (103: 105: 107: 109) sts.
Cont straight until sleeve measures 45 (45: 45: 46: 46) cm, ending with a WS row.
Shape raglan
Cast off 8 sts at beg of next 2 rows.
85 (87: 89: 91: 93) sts.***
Dec 1 st at each end of next and every foll 4th row until 75 (77: 79: 81: 83) sts rem, then on every foll alt row until 21 sts rem.
Work 1 row, ending with a WS row.
Left sleeve only
Dec 1 st at each end of next row. 19 sts.
Cast off 6 sts at beg of next row. 13 sts.
Dec 1 st at beg of next row. 12 sts.
Cast off 6 sts at beg of next row.
Right sleeve only
Cast off 7 sts at beg and dec 1 st at end of next row. 13 sts.
Work 1 row. Cast off 6 sts at beg and dec 1 st at end of next row. 6 sts.
Work 1 row.
Both sleeves
Cast off rem 6 sts.

Sweater

BACK and FRONT (both alike)
Work as given for back of cardigan to **, using colours as folls: use yarn A in place of yarn A, and yarn B in place of **both** yarn B **and** yarn C.
Extra small size only
Next row (RS): K2, K2tog tbl, yfwd, K2tog, K to last 6 sts, K2tog tbl, yfwd, K2tog, K2.
Next row: Purl.
Next row: K2, K2tog tbl, yfwd, K to last 4 sts, yfwd, K2tog, K2.
Next row: Purl.
Rep last 4 rows twice more. 97 sts.
Medium, large and extra large sizes only
Next row (RS): K2, K2tog tbl, yfwd, K3tog, K to last 7 sts, K3tog tbl, yfwd, K2tog, K2.
Next row: Purl.
Rep last 2 rows – (-: 2: 5: 8) times more.
– (-: 107: 103: 99) sts.
All sizes
Next row (RS): K2, K2tog tbl, yfwd, K2tog, K to last 6 sts, K2tog tbl, yfwd, K2tog, K2.
Next row: Purl.
Rep last 2 rows 26 (33: 31: 29: 27) times more.
Leave rem 43 sts on a holder.

SLEEVES (both alike)
Work as given for sleeves of cardigan to ***, using colours as folls: use yarn A in place of yarn A, and yarn B in place of **both** yarn B **and** yarn C.
Next row (RS): K2, K2tog tbl, yfwd, K2tog, K to last 6 sts, K2tog tbl, yfwd, K2tog, K2.
Next row: Purl.

(Knitting instructions continued on page 56)

ISLA

Continued from page 55

Next row: K2, K2tog tbl, yfwd, K to last 4 sts, yfwd, K2tog, K2.
Next row: Purl.
Rep last 4 rows twice more. 79 (81: 83: 85: 87) sts.
Next row (RS): K2, K2tog tbl, yfwd, K2tog, K to last 6 sts, K2tog tbl, yfwd, K2tog, K2.
Next row: Purl.
Rep last 2 rows 26 (27: 28: 29: 30) times more. Leave rem 25 sts on a holder.

MAKING UP
PRESS all pieces as described on the information page.

Cardigan
Join raglan seams using back stitch, or mattress stitch if preferred.
Neck border
With RS facing, 2¼mm (US 1) needles and yarn A, pick up and knit 20 (22: 22: 24: 24) sts up right side of neck, 17 sts from right sleeve, 31 (33: 33: 35: 35) sts from back, 17 sts from left sleeve, and 20 (22: 22: 24: 24) sts down left side of neck. 105 (111: 111: 117: 117) sts.
Row 1 (WS): K3, *P3, K3, rep from * to end.
Row 2: P3, *K3, P3, rep from * to end.
Rep last 2 rows once more. Cast off in rib.

Right front border
With RS facing, 2¼mm (US 1) needles and yarn A, pick up and knit 149 sts evenly along right front opening edge, between cast-on edge and top of neck border.
Row 1 (WS): K1, P3, *K3, P3, rep from * to last st, K1.
Row 2: K4, *P3, K3, rep from * to last st, K1.
Rep last 2 rows once more.
Cast off in rib.
Left front border
With RS facing, 2¼mm (US 1) needles and yarn B, pick up and knit 149 sts evenly along left front opening edge, between top of neck border and cast-on edge.
Work 4 rows in rib as given for right front border, making buttonholes in 4th row as folls:
Row 4 (RS) (buttonhole row): Rib 1, *cast off 2 sts, rib until there are 10 sts on right needle after cast-off, rep from * to last 4 sts, cast off 2 sts, rib to end.
Row 5 (WS): Cast off first 2 sts (one st on right needle), *turn (one st now on left needle), (K this st and slip it back onto left needle) twice, turn and cast off 10 sts (one st on right needle), rep from * to end, noting that there is only 1 st to cast off at end of last rep.
Sew on buttons to inside of right front along pick up row of border.
Sweater
Join both front and right back raglan seams using back stitch, or mattress stitch if preferred.

(Knitting instructions continued on page 86)

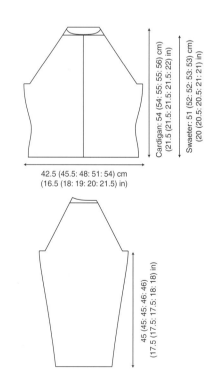

Cardigan: 54 (54: 55: 55: 56) cm (21.5 (21.5: 21.5: 21.5: 22) in)
Sweater: 51 (52: 52: 53: 53) cm (20 (20.5: 20.5: 21: 21) in)

42.5 (45.5: 48: 51: 54) cm
(16.5 (18: 19: 20: 21.5) in)

45 (45: 45: 46: 46) (17.5 (17.5: 17.5: 18: 18) in)

Isla Sweater knitted in Rowanspun 4 ply & Lurex Shimmer, Heather Cardigan knitted in Kid Classic, knitting instructions on page 14

CALUM

YARN

Rowan Rowanspun Aran

	S	M	L	XL	XXL	
To fit chest	97	102	107	112	117	cm
	38	40	42	44	46	in
Sweater	6	7	7	7	8	x 100gm
Jacket	7	7	8	8	8	x 100gm

(sweater photographed in Midnight 965, jacket in Shark 963)

NEEDLES

1 pair 5mm (no 6) (US 8) needles
1 pair 5½mm (no 5) (US 9) needles

ZIP - 10 cm zip for sweater, or 66 cm open ended zip for jacket

TENSION

16 sts and 23 rows to 10 cm measured over stocking stitch using 5½mm (US 9) needles.

Sweater

BACK

Cast on 89 (93: 97: 101: 105) sts using 5mm (US 8) needles.
Row 1 (RS): K1 (3: 0: 0: 2), P3 (3: 1: 3: 3), *K4, P3, rep from * to last 1 (3: 5: 0: 2) sts, K1 (3: 4: 0: 2), P0 (0: 1: 0: 0).
Row 2: P1 (3: 0: 0: 2), K3 (3: 1: 3: 3), *P4, K3, rep from * to last 1 (3: 5: 0: 2) sts, P1 (3: 4: 0: 2), K0 (0: 1: 0: 0).
These 2 rows form rib.
Work in rib for a further 16 rows.
Change to 5½mm (US 9) needles.
Beg with a K row, work in st st until back measures 37 cm, ending with a WS row.

Shape raglan armholes

Cast off 4 sts at beg of next 2 rows.
81 (85: 89: 93: 97) sts.
Dec 1 st at each end of next 7 (7: 9: 9: 9) rows, then on every foll alt row until 21 (23: 23: 25: 27) sts rem.
Work 1 row, ending with a WS row. Cast off.

FRONT

Work as given for back until 63 (65: 65: 67: 69) sts rem in raglan shaping.
Work 1 row, ending with a WS row.

Divide for front opening

Next row (RS): K2tog, K29 (30: 30: 31: 32) and turn, leaving rem sts on a holder.
30 (31: 31: 32: 33) sts.
Work each side of neck separately.
Next row (WS): K1, P to end.
This row sets the sts – neck opening edge st worked as a K st on every row with all other sts in st st.
Cont as set, dec 1 st at raglan edge on next and every foll alt row until 19 (20: 20: 21: 22) sts rem, ending with a RS row.

Shape neck

Next row (WS): Patt 5 (6: 6: 7: 8) sts and slip these sts onto a holder, P to end. 14 sts.

Shona Sweater knitted in Rowanspun DK, knitting instructions on page 60, Johnstone Gloves knitted in Rowanspun DK & Kidsilk Haze, knitting instructions on page 50 & Calum Jacket knitted in Rowanspun Aran

Dec 1 st at neck edge on next 3 rows, then on foll 2 alt rows **and at same time** dec 1 st at raglan edge on next and every foll alt row. 5 sts.
Work 1 row.
Dec 1 st at raglan edge on next and foll 2 alt rows **and at same time** dec 1 st at neck edge on 3rd row. 1 st.
Next row (WS): P1 and fasten off.
With RS facing, rejoin yarn to rem sts, K2tog, K to last 2 sts, K2tog.
Work to match first side, reversing shapings.

SLEEVES (both alike)

Cast on 53 (53: 55: 57: 57) sts using 5mm (US 8) needles.
Row 1 (RS): P0 (0: 1: 2: 2), *K4, P3, rep from * to last 4 (4: 5: 6: 6) sts, K4, P0 (0: 1: 2: 2).
Row 2: K0 (0: 1: 2: 2), *P4, K3, rep from * to last 4 (4: 5: 6: 6) sts, P4, K0 (0: 1: 2: 2).
These 2 rows form rib.
Work in rib for a further 8 rows.
Change to 5½mm (US 9) needles.
Cont in rib, shaping sides by inc 1 st at each end of next and every foll 10th row to 69 (63: 65: 69: 61) sts, then on every foll 8th row until there are 75 (77: 79: 81: 83) sts, taking inc sts into rib.
Cont straight until sleeve measures 50 (51: 51: 52: 52) cm, ending with a WS row.

Shape raglan

Cast off 4 sts at beg of next 2 rows.
67 (69: 71: 73: 75) sts.
Dec 1 st at each end of next 5 rows, then on every foll alt row until 13 sts rem.
Work 1 row, ending with a WS row.

Left sleeve only

Dec 1 st at each end of next row. 11 sts.
Cast off 3 sts at beg of next row. 8 sts.
Dec 1 st at beg of next row. 7 sts.
Cast off 4 sts at beg of foll row. 3 sts.

Right sleeve only

Cast off 4 sts at beg and dec 1 st at end of next row. 8 sts.
Work 1 row. Rep last 2 rows once more. 3 sts.

Both sleeves

Cast off rem 3 sts.

Jacket

BACK

Work as given for back of sweater.

LEFT FRONT

Cast on 46 (48: 50: 52: 54) sts using 5mm (US 8) needles.
Row 1 (RS): K1 (3: 0: 0: 2), P3 (3: 1: 3: 3), *K4, P3, rep from * to end.
Row 2: K3, *P4, K3, rep from * to last 1 (3: 5: 0: 2) sts, P1 (3: 4: 0: 2), K0 (0: 1: 0: 0).
These 2 rows form rib.
Work in rib for a further 16 rows.
Change to 5½mm (US 9) needles.
Beg with a K row, work in st st until left front matches back to beg of raglan armhole shaping, ending with a WS row.

Shape raglan armhole

Cast off 4 sts at beg of next row. 42 (44: 46: 48: 50) sts.
Work 1 row.
Dec 1 st at raglan edge of next 7 (7: 9: 9: 9) rows, then on every foll alt row until 19 (20: 21: 22: 23) sts rem, ending with a RS row.

Shape neck

Cast off 6 (7: 6: 7: 8) sts at beg of next row.
13 (13: 15: 15: 15) sts.
Dec 1 st at neck edge on next 4 rows **and at same time** dec 1 st at raglan edge on next and foll alt row. 7 (7: 9: 9: 9) sts.
Dec 1 st at each end of next and foll 2 (2: 3: 3: 3) alt rows. 1 st.
Next row (WS): P1 and fasten off.

RIGHT FRONT

Cast on 46 (48: 50: 52: 54) sts using 5mm (US 8) needles.
Row 1 (RS): P3, *K4, P3, rep from * to last 1 (3: 5: 0: 2) sts, K1 (3: 4: 0: 2), P0 (0: 1: 0: 0).
Row 2: P1 (3: 0: 0: 2), K3 (3: 1: 3: 3), *P4, K3, rep from * to end.
These 2 rows form rib.
Complete to match left front, reversing shapings.

SLEEVES (both alike)

Work as given for sleeves of sweater.

MAKING UP

PRESS all pieces as described on the info page.
Sweater
Join raglan seams using back stitch, or mattress stitch if preferred.
Collar
With RS facing and 5mm (US 8) needles, K across 5 (6: 6: 7: 8) sts on right front holder, pick up and knit 16 (15: 15: 15: 17) sts up right side of neck, 9 sts from right sleeve, 21 (21: 21: 26: 27) sts from back, 9 sts from left sleeve, and 16 (15: 15: 15: 17) sts down left side of neck, then K across 5 (6: 6: 7: 8) sts on left front holder. 81 (81: 81: 88: 95) sts.
Row 1: K1, P3, *K3, P4, rep from * to last 7 sts, K3, P3, K1.
Row 2: K4, *P3, K4, rep from * to end.
Rep last 2 rows until collar measures 10 cm.
Cast off in rib.

(Knitting instructions continued on page 88)

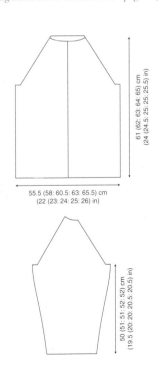

61 (62: 63: 64: 65) cm
(24 (24.5: 25: 25: 25.5) in)

55.5 (58: 60.5: 63: 65.5) cm
(22 (23: 24: 25: 26) in)

50 (51: 51: 52: 52) cm
(19.5 (20: 20: 20.5: 20.5) in)

SHONA

YARN
Rowan Rowanspun DK

	XS	S	M	L	XL
To fit bust	81	86	91	97	102 cm
	32	34	36	38	40 in
A Eau de nil 735	3	3	4	4	4 x 50gm
B Lavender 733	3	3	4	4	4 x 50gm

NEEDLES
1 pair 3¼mm (no 10) (US 3) needles
1 pair 4mm (no 8) (US 6) needles

TENSION
21 sts and 29 rows to 10 cm measured over stocking stitch using 4mm (US 6) needles.

BACK
Cast on 85 (91: 97: 103: 109) sts using 3¼mm (US 3) needles and yarn A.
Row 1 (RS): K2, *P3, K3, rep from * to last 5 sts, P3, K2.
Row 2: P2, *K3, P3, rep from * to last 5 sts, K3, P2.
These 2 rows form rib.
Work in rib for a further 12 rows, ending with a WS row.
Change to 4mm (US 6) needles.
Beg with a K row, work in st st as folls:
Using yarn A, work 2 rows.
Join in yarn B and work in 28 row stripe sequence as folls:
Using yarn B, work 2 rows.
Using yarn B, dec 1 st at each end of next and foll 6th row.
81 (87: 93: 99: 105) sts.
Work a further 5 rows using yarn B, completing 14 rows using yarn B and ending with a WS row.
Change to yarn A.
Using yarn A, dec 1 st at each end of next and every foll 6th row until 75 (81: 87: 93: 99) sts rem.
Work 1 more row using yarn A, completing 14 rows using yarn A and ending with a WS row.
Last 28 rows form stripe sequence.
Keeping stripe sequence correct, cont as folls:
Work 4 rows.
Dec 1 st at each end of next row.
73 (79: 85: 91: 97) sts.
Work 9 rows, ending with a WS row.
Inc 1 st at each end of next and every foll 6th row until there are 89 (95: 101: 107: 113) sts.
Work 11 rows, ending after 12 rows using yarn B and with a WS row.
(Back measures approx 38 cm.)
Shape raglan armholes
Keeping stripe sequence correct, cast off 4 sts at beg of next 2 rows.
81 (87: 93: 99: 105) sts.
Extra small size only
Next row (RS): P2, K2tog, K to last 4 sts, K2tog tbl, P2. 79 sts.
Next row: K2, P to last 2 sts, K2.
Next row: P2, K to last 2 sts, P2.
Next row: K2, P to last 2 sts, K2.
Medium, large and extra large sizes only
Next row (RS): P2, K3tog, K to last 5 sts, K3tog tbl, P2.
Next row: K2, P to last 2 sts, K2.
Rep last 2 rows – (-: 1: 2: 4) times more.
– (-: 85: 87: 85) sts.

All sizes
Next row (RS): P2, K2tog, K to last 4 sts, K2tog tbl, P2.
Next row: K2, P to last 2 sts, K2.
Rep last 2 rows 26 (29: 28: 28: 27) times more.
Cast off rem 25 (27: 27: 29: 29) sts.

FRONT
Work as given for back until 39 (41: 41: 45: 45) sts rem in raglan shaping.
Work 1 row, ending with a WS row.
Shape neck
Next row (RS): P2, K2tog, K7 (7: 7: 9: 9) and turn, leaving rem sts on a holder.
Work each side of neck separately.
Work 1 row.
Working all **raglan** decreases 2 sts in from end of row as set, dec 1 st at each end of next and every foll alt row until 4 sts rem.
Next row (WS): P2, K2.
Next row: P1, P3tog.
Next row: K2.
Next row: P2tog and fasten off.
With RS facing, rejoin yarn to rem sts, cast off centre 17 (19: 19: 19: 19) sts, K to last 4 sts, K2tog tbl, P2.
Work to match first side, reversing shapings.

SLEEVES
Cast on 45 (47: 49: 51: 53) sts using 3¼mm (US 3) needles and yarn B.
Row 1 (RS): P0 (1: 2: 3: 4), K3, *P3, K3, rep from * to last 0 (1: 2: 3: 4) sts, P0 (1: 2: 3: 4).
Row 2: K0 (1: 2: 3: 4), P3, *K3, P3, rep from * to last 0 (1: 2: 3: 4) sts, K0 (1: 2: 3: 4).
These 2 rows form rib.
Work in rib for a further 12 rows, ending with a WS row.
Change to 4mm (US 6) needles.
Beg with a K row, work in st st as folls:
Using yarn B, work 2 rows.
Join in yarn A.
Beg with 14 rows using yarn A, cont in 28 row stripe sequence as given for back, shaping sides by inc 1 st at each end of 3rd and every foll 8th row until there are 71 (73: 75: 77: 79) sts.
Work 11 rows, ending after 12 rows using yarn B and with a WS row.
(Sleeve measures approx 43 cm.)
Shape raglan
Keeping stripe sequence correct, cast off 4 sts at beg of next 2 rows. 63 (65: 67: 69: 71) sts.
Next row (RS): P2, K2tog, K to last 4 sts, K2tog tbl, P2.
Next row: K2, P to last 2 sts, K2.
Rep last 2 rows 26 (27: 28: 29: 30) times more.
9 sts.
Left sleeve only
Next row (RS): P2, K2tog, K1, K2tog tbl, P2.
7 sts.
Cast off 2 sts at beg of next row. 5 sts.
Next row: P2, K2tog, K1.
Cast off 2 sts at beg of next row.
Right sleeve only
Next row (RS): Cast off 3 sts, K to last 4 sts, K2tog tbl, P2.
Work 1 row.
Cast off 3 sts at beg of next row.
Work 1 row.

Both sleeves
Cast off rem 2 sts.

MAKING UP
PRESS all pieces as described on the info page.
Join both front and right back raglan seams using back stitch, or mattress stitch if preferred.
Neckband
With RS facing, 3¼mm (US 3) needles and yarn A, pick up and knit 6 sts from top of left sleeve, 7 (8: 8: 10: 10) sts down left side of neck, 17 (19: 19: 19: 19) sts from front, 7 (8: 8: 10: 10) sts up right side of neck, 6 sts from top of right sleeve, then 25 (27: 27: 29: 29) sts from back.
68 (74: 74: 80: 80) sts.
Row 1 (WS): K1, *K3, P3, rep from * to last st, P1.
Rep this row until neckband measures 10 cm.
Cast off in rib.
See information page for finishing instructions.

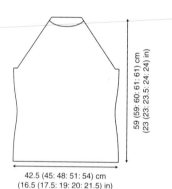

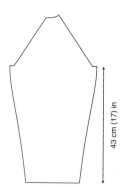

42.5 (45: 48: 51: 54) cm
(16.5 (17.5: 19: 20: 21.5) in)

59 (59: 60: 61: 61) cm
(23 (23: 23.5: 24: 24) in)

43 cm (17) in

Shona Sweater knitted in Rowanspun DK, Johnstone Gloves knitted in Rowanspun DK & Kidsilk Haze, knitting instructions on page 50 & Calum Jacket knitted in Rowanspun Aran, knitting instructions on page 59

BETH

YARN

Rowan Rowanspun 4 ply

	XS	S	M	L	XL	
To fit bust	81	86	91	97	102cm	
	32	34	36	38	40 in	
A Jade	712	2	2	2	2	x 25gm
B Midnight	708	6	7	7	8	8 x 25gm

NEEDLES

1 pair 2¼mm (no 13) (US 1) needles
1 pair 3mm (no 11) (US 2/3) needles

BUTTONS – 9

TENSION

28 sts and 40 rows to 10 cm measured over
stocking stitch using 3mm (US 2/3) needles.

BACK

Cast on 98 (106: 114: 122: 130) sts using 2¼mm
(US 1) needles and yarn A.
Row 1 (RS): K2, *P2, K2, rep from * to end.
Row 2: P2, *K2, P2, rep from * to end.
These 2 rows form rib.
Work in rib for a further 32 rows, inc 1 st at
centre of last row and ending with a WS row.
99 (107: 115: 123: 131) sts.
Break off yarn A and join in yarn B.
Change to 3mm (US 2/3) needles.
Beg with a K row, cont in st st, as folls:
Work 10 rows.
Next row (RS) (inc): K3, M1, K to last 3 sts,
M1, K3.
Working all increases 3 sts in from ends of rows
as set by last row, inc 1 st at each end of every foll
10th row until there are 113 (121: 129: 137: 145) sts.

Cont straight until back measures 28 (29: 29: 30:
30) cm, ending with a WS row.
Shape armholes
Cast off 4 (4: 4: 6: 6) sts at beg of next 2 rows.
105 (113: 121: 125: 133) sts.
Next row (RS) (dec): K3, K3tog, K to last 6
sts, K3tog tbl, K3.
Working all decreases as set by last row, cont as
folls:
Work 1 row.
Dec 2 sts at each end of next and foll 0 (1: 2: 2:
3) alt rows, then on every foll 4th row until
89 (93: 97: 101: 105) sts rem.
Cont straight until armhole measures 20 (20: 21:
21: 22) cm, ending with a WS row.
Shape shoulders and back neck
Cast off 8 (8: 9: 9: 10) sts at beg of next 2 rows.
73 (77: 79: 83: 85) sts.
Next row (RS): Cast off 8 (8: 9: 9: 10) sts, K
until there are 11 (12: 12: 13: 13) sts on right
needle and turn, leaving rem sts on a holder.
Work each side of neck separately.
Cast off 4 sts at beg of next row.
Cast off rem 7 (8: 8: 9: 9) sts.
With RS facing, rejoin yarn to rem sts, cast off
centre 35 (37: 37: 39: 39) sts, K to end.
Work to match first side, reversing shapings.

LEFT FRONT

Cast on 52 (56: 60: 64: 68) sts using 2¼mm (US 1)
needles and yarn A.
Row 1 (RS): K2, *P2, K2, rep from * to last 6 sts,
(K1, P1) 3 times.
Row 2: (P1, K1) 3 times, P2, *K2, P2, rep from
* to end.
These 2 rows set the sts – front opening edge 6 sts
in moss st with all other sts in rib.
Keeping sts correct, work a further 31 rows,
ending with a RS row.
Row 34 (WS): Moss st 6 sts and slip these sts
onto a holder, M1, rib to last st, inc in last st.
48 (52: 56: 60: 64) sts.
Break off yarn A and join in yarn B.
Change to 3mm (US 2/3) needles.
Beg with a K row, cont in st st, as folls:
Work 10 rows.
Next row (RS) (inc): K3, M1, K to end.
Working all increases 3 sts in from beg of row as
set by last row, inc 1 st at beg of every foll 10th
row until there are 55 (59: 63: 67: 71) sts.
Cont straight until left front matches back to
beg of armhole shaping, ending with a WS row.
Shape armhole
Cast off 4 (4: 4: 6: 6) sts at beg of next row.
51 (55: 59: 61: 65) sts.
Work 1 row.
Next row (RS) (dec): K3, K3tog, K to end.
Working all decreases as set by last row, cont as
folls:
Work 1 row.
Dec 2 sts at armhole edge of next and foll 0 (1:
2: 2: 3) alt rows, then on every foll 4th row until
43 (45: 47: 49: 51) sts rem.
Cont straight until 31 (31: 31: 33: 33) rows less
have been worked than on back to start of
shoulder shaping, ending with a RS row.
Shape neck
Cast off 8 (9: 9: 9: 9) sts at beg of next row, then
4 sts at beg of foll alt row. 31 (32: 34: 36: 38) sts.

Dec 1 st at neck edge of next 3 rows, then on
foll 2 (2: 2: 3: 3) alt rows, then on every foll 4th
row until 23 (24: 26: 27: 29) sts rem.
Work 9 rows, ending with a WS row.
Shape shoulder
Cast off 8 (8: 9: 9: 10) sts at beg of next and foll
alt row.
Work 1 row.
Cast off rem 7 (8: 8: 9: 9) sts.

RIGHT FRONT

Cast on 52 (56: 60: 64: 68) sts using 2¼mm (US 1)
needles and yarn A.
Row 1 (RS): (P1, K1) 3 times, K2, *P2, K2, rep
from * to end.
Row 2: P2, *K2, P2, rep from * to last 6 sts,
(K1, P1) 3 times.
These 2 rows set the sts – front opening edge 6 sts
in moss st with all other sts in rib.
Keeping sts correct, work a further 2 rows,
ending with a WS row.
Row 5 (RS): Moss st 3 sts, yrn (to make a
buttonhole), work 2 tog, patt to end.
Work 25 rows, ending with a WS row.
Row 31: As row 5.
Work a further 2 rows, ending with a RS row.
Row 34 (WS): Inc in first st, rib to last 6 sts,
M1 and turn, leaving last 6 sts on a holder.
48 (52: 56: 60: 64) sts.
Break off yarn A and join in yarn B.
Change to 3mm (US 2/3) needles.
Beg with a K row, cont in st st, as folls:
Work 10 rows.
Next row (RS) (inc): K to last 3 sts, M1, K3.
Working all increases 3 sts in from end of row as
set by last row, inc 1 st at end of every foll 10th
row until there are 55 (59: 63: 67: 71) sts.
Complete to match left front, reversing shapings.

(Knitting instructions continued on page 88)

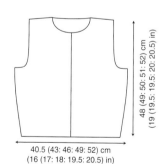

40.5 (43: 46: 49: 52) cm
(16 (17: 18: 19.5: 20.5) in)

48 (49: 50: 51: 52) cm
(19 (19.5: 19.5: 20: 20.5) in)

44 (44: 44: 45: 45) cm
(17.5 (17.5: 17.5: 17.5: 17.5) in)

YARN

Rowan Rowanspun Aran

	XS	S	M	L	XL
To fit bust	81	86	91	97	102cm
	32	34	36	38	40 in
	9	9	10	10	11 x 100gm

(photographed in Shark 963)

NEEDLES

1 pair 5mm (no 6) (US 8) needles
1 pair 5½mm (no 5) (US 9) needles

BUTTONS - 8

TENSION

15 sts and 26 rows to 10 cm measured over moss stitch using 5½mm (US 9) needles.

BACK

Lower back

Cast on 79 (83: 87: 91: 95) sts using 5mm (US 8) needles.
Row 1 (RS): K1, *P1, K1, rep from * to end.
Row 2: As row 1.
These 2 rows form moss st.
Work in moss st for a further 18 rows, ending with a WS row.
Change to 5½mm (US 9) needles.
Cont straight until lower back measures 60 cm, ending with a WS row.
Cast off in moss st.

Upper back

Cast on 79 (83: 87: 91: 95) sts using 5½mm (US 9) needles.
Work in moss st as given for lower back until upper back measures 11 cm, ending with a WS row.

Shape raglan armholes

Cast off 4 sts at beg of next 2 rows.
71 (75: 79: 83: 87) sts.
Dec 1 st at each end of next 1 (1: 3: 3: 5) rows, then on every foll alt row until 17 (19: 19: 21: 21) sts rem.
Work 1 row, ending with a WS row.
Cast off in moss st.

POCKET LININGS (make 2)

Cast on 21 sts using 5½mm (US 9) needles.
Row 1 (RS): P1, *K1, P1, rep from * to end.
Row 2: As row 1.
These 2 rows form moss st.
Work in moss st for a further 28 rows, ending with a WS row.
Break yarn and leave sts on a holder.

LEFT FRONT

Lower left front

Cast on 44 (46: 48: 50: 52) sts using 5mm (US 8) needles.
Row 1 (RS): *K1, P1, rep from * to end.
Row 2: *P1, K1, rep from * to end.
These 2 rows form moss st.

Thistle Coat knitted in Rowanspun Aran worn over Elizabeth Sweater knitted in Kidsilk Haze, knitting instructions on page 25 & Cameron Sweater knitted in Rowanspun Aran, knitting instructions on page 8

Work in moss st for a further 18 rows, ending with a WS row.
Change to 5½mm (US 9) needles.
Cont straight until lower left front measures 33 cm, ending with a WS row.

Work side and pocket back

Next row (RS): Moss st 13 (15: 17: 19: 21) sts, slip rem 31 sts on a holder and, in their place, moss st across 21 sts of first pocket lining. 34 (36: 38: 40: 42) sts.
Work a further 38 rows on these sts, ending with a RS row.
Break yarn and leave sts on a second holder.

Work pocket front

With RS facing, rejoin yarn to 31 sts left on first holder and work in moss st for 39 rows, ending with a RS row.

Join sections

Next row (WS): Moss st first 10 sts of pocket front, with RS of pocket back against WS of pocket front work tog first st of pocket back with next st of pocket front, work tog next 20 sts of pocket back with rem 20 sts of pocket front, moss st rem 13 (15: 17: 19: 21) sts of side and pocket back section. 44 (46: 48: 50: 52) sts.
Cont straight until lower left front measures 60 cm, ending with a WS row.
Cast off in moss st.

Upper left front

Cast on 44 (46: 48: 50: 52) sts using 5½mm (US 9) needles.
Work in moss st as given for lower left front until upper left front measures 11 cm, ending with a WS row.

Shape raglan armhole

Cast off 4 sts at beg of next row.
40 (42: 44: 46: 48) sts.
Work 1 row.
Dec 1 st at raglan edge of next 1 (1: 3: 3: 5) rows, then on every foll alt row until 20 (21: 21: 23: 23) sts rem, ending with a RS row.

Shape neck

Cast off 10 (11: 11: 11: 11) sts at beg of next row. 10 (10: 10: 12: 12) sts.
Dec 1 st at each end of next and every foll alt row until 4 sts rem.
Work 1 row, ending with a WS row.
Dec 1 st at raglan edge only on next and foll alt row.
Work 1 row, ending with a WS row.
Next row (RS): Work 2 tog and fasten off.
Holding pieces with WS together (so that seam is on RS), join cast-on edge of upper left front to cast-off edge of lower left front using back stitch.
Mark positions for 8 buttons along left front opening edge – first to come 27 cm up from cast-on edge, last to come 1 cm below neck shaping and rem 6 buttons evenly spaced between.

RIGHT FRONT

Lower right front

Cast on 44 (46: 48: 50: 52) sts using 5mm (US 8) needles.
Row 1 (RS): *P1, K1, rep from * to end.
Row 2: *K1, P1, rep from * to end.
These 2 rows form moss st.
Work in moss st for a further 18 rows, ending with a WS row.
Change to 5½mm (US 9) needles.

Cont straight until lower right front measures 27 cm, ending with a WS row.
Next row (buttonhole row) (RS): Moss st 4 sts, cast off 2 sts (for first buttonhole – on next row, cast on 2 sts over these cast-off sts), moss st to end.
Making a further 7 buttonholes in same way as first and noting that no further reference will be made to buttonholes, cont as folls:
Cont straight until lower right front measures 33 cm, ending with a WS row.

Work pocket front

Next row (RS): Moss st to last 13 (15: 17: 19: 21) sts and turn, leaving rem 13 (15: 17: 19: 21) sts on a holder.
Work in moss st on these 31 sts for a further 38 rows, ending with a RS row.
Break yarn and leave sts on a second holder.

Work side and pocket back

Next row (RS): Moss st across 21 sts of second pocket lining, then moss st across 13 (15: 17: 19: 21) sts left on first holder. 34 (36: 38: 40: 42) sts.
Work a further 38 rows on these sts, ending with a RS row.

Join sections

Next row (WS): Moss st first 13 (15: 17: 19: 21) sts of side and pocket back section, with RS of pocket back against WS of pocket front work tog next st of pocket back with first st of pocket front, work tog rem 20 sts of pocket back with next 20 sts of pocket front, moss st rem 10 sts of pocket front. 44 (46: 48: 50: 52) sts.
Cont straight until lower right front measures 60 cm, ending with a WS row.
Cast off in moss st.

(Knitting instructions continued on page 89)

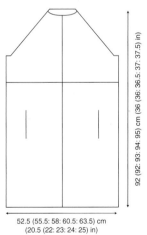

92 (92: 93: 94: 95) cm (36 (36: 36.5: 37: 37.5) in)

52.5 (55.5: 58: 60.5: 63.5) cm (20.5 (22: 23: 24: 25) in)

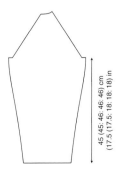

45 (45: 46: 46: 46) cm (17.5 (17.5: 18: 18: 18) in)

FIFE

YARN
Rowan Rowanspun DK

	XS	S	M	L	XL
To fit bust	81	86	91	97	102cm
	32	34	36	38	40 in
	6	7	7	8	8 x 50gm

(photographed in Snowball 730)

NEEDLES
1 pair 3¾mm (no 9) (US 5) needles
1 pair 4mm (no 8) (US 6) needles
Cable needle

TENSION
21 sts and 29 rows to 10 cm measured over
stocking stitch using 4mm (US 8) needles.

SPECIAL ABBREVIATIONS
C8F = Cable 8 front Slip next 4 sts onto cable
needle and leave at front of work, K4, then K4
from cable needle.

C8B = Cable 8 back Slip next 4 sts onto cable
needle and leave at back of work, K4, then K4
from cable needle.

C4F = Cable 4 front Slip next 3 sts onto cable
needle and leave at front of work, K1, then K3
from cable needle.

C4B = Cable 4 back Slip next st onto cable
needle and leave at back of work, K3, then K1
from cable needle.

Cr4R = Cross 4 right Slip next st onto cable
needle and leave at back of work, K3, then P1
from cable needle.

Cr4L = Cross 4 left Slip next 3 sts onto cable
needle and leave at front of work, P1, then K3
from cable needle.

BACK
Cast on 100 (106: 112: 118: 124) sts using 3¾mm
(US 5) needles.
Row 1 (RS): P4 (0: 2: 0: 0), K3 (2: 3: 0: 3), (P5, K3)
4 (5: 5: 6: 6) times, P3, K16, P3, (K3, P5) 4 (5: 5: 6: 6)
times, K3 (2: 3: 0: 3), P4 (0: 2: 0: 0).
Row 2: K4 (0: 2: 0: 0), P3 (2: 3: 0: 3), (K5, P3) 4 (5:
5: 6: 6) times, K3, P16, K3, (P3, K5) 4 (5: 5: 6: 6) times,
P3 (2: 3: 0: 3), K4 (0: 2: 0: 0).
Rep last 2 rows 7 times more, inc 1 st at each end
of last row. 102 (108: 114: 120: 126) sts.
Change to 4mm (US 6) needles.
Starting and ending rows as indicated and
repeating the 16 row repeat throughout, cont in
patt foll chart as folls:
Inc 1 st at each end of 9th and every foll 8th row
to 108 (114: 120: 126: 132) sts, then on every foll
6th row until there are 114 (120: 126: 132: 138) sts,
taking inc sts into patt.

Cont straight until back measures 24 cm, ending
with a WS row.
Shape raglan armholes
Keeping patt correct, cast off 6 sts at beg of next
2 rows. 102 (108: 114: 120: 126) sts.
Dec 1 st at each end of next 11 (15: 19: 23: 27) rows,
then on every foll alt row until 32 sts rem.
Work 1 row, dec 3sts evenly.
Leave rem 29 sts on a holder.

FRONT
Work as given for back until 46 sts rem in raglan
shaping.
Work 1 row, ending with a WS row.
Shape neck
Next row (RS): Work 2 tog, patt 10 sts and turn,
leaving rem sts on a holder.
Work each side of neck separately.
Dec 1 st at neck edge of next row. 10 sts.
Dec 1 st at each end of next and foll 3 alt rows.
2 sts.
Work 1 row, ending with a WS row.
Next row (RS): Work 2 tog and fasten off.
With RS facing, slip centre 22 sts onto a holder,
rejoin yarn to rem sts, patt to last 2 sts, work 2 tog.
Work to match first side, reversing shapings.

SLEEVES (both alike)
Cast on 64 (64: 66: 68: 68) sts using 3¾mm (US 5)
needles.
Row 1 (RS): P2 (2: 3: 4: 4), K3, (P5, K3) twice,
P3, K16, P3, (K3, P5) twice, K3, P2 (2: 3: 4: 4).
Row 2: K2 (2: 3: 4: 4), P3, (K5, P3) twice, K3,
P16, K3, (P3, K5) twice, P3, K2 (2: 3: 4: 4).
Rep last 2 rows 7 times more, inc 1 st at each
end of last row. 66 (66: 68: 70: 70) sts.
Change to 4mm (US 6) needles.
Starting and ending rows as indicated and
repeating the 16 row repeat throughout, cont in
patt foll chart as folls:
Inc 1 st at each end of 11th and every foll 10th
row to 86 (78: 82: 84: 76) sts, then on every foll
8th row until there are 88 (90: 92: 94: 96) sts,
taking inc sts into patt.
Cont straight until sleeve measures 46 (46: 47:
47: 47) cm, ending with a WS row.
Shape raglan
Keeping patt correct, cast off 6 sts at beg of next
2 rows. 76 (78: 80: 82: 84) sts.
Dec 1 st at each end of next and every foll 4th
row until 68 (70: 72: 74: 76) sts rem, then on
every foll alt row until 26 sts rem.
Work 1 row, ending with a WS row.
Left sleeve only
Dec 1 st at each end of next row. 24 sts.
Cast off 7 sts at beg of next row. 17 sts.

Dec 1 st at beg of next row. 16 sts.
Cast off 8 sts at beg of next row. 8 sts.
Right sleeve only
Cast off 8 sts at beg and dec 1 st at end of next
row.
Work 1 row.
Rep last 2 rows once more. 8 sts.
Both sleeves
Cast off rem 8 sts.

MAKING UP
PRESS all pieces as described on the info page.
Join both front and right back raglan seams using
back stitch, or mattress stitch if preferred.
Neckband
With RS facing and 3¾mm (US 5) needles, pick
up and knit 23 sts from left sleeve, 15 sts down
left side of neck, patt across 22 sts from front
holder, pick up and knit 15 sts up right side of
neck, 23 sts from right sleeve, then 29 sts from
back. 127 sts.
Row 1 (WS): P3, (K5, P3) 8 times, K3, patt 16 sts,
K3, P3, (K5, P3) 4 times, K3.
Row 2: P3, (K3, P5) 4 times, K3, P3, patt 16 sts,
P3, (K3, P5) 8 times, K3.
Rep last 2 rows for 4 cm.
Cast off in patt.
See information page for finishing instructions.

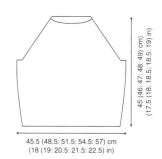

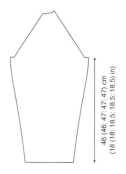

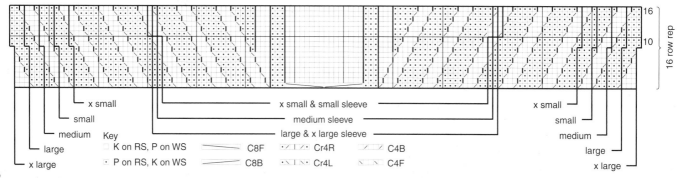

YARN

Rowan Rowanspun Chunky, Kid Classic and Rowanspun DK

	XS	S	M	L	XL	
To fit bust	81	86	91	97	102	cm
	32	34	36	38	40	in

Fairisle cardigan

Rowanspun Chunky

		XS	S	M	L	XL	
A	Silver	984 5	6	6	6	7	x100gm

Kid Classic★

B	Smoke	831 2	2	2	3	3	x 50gm

Rowanspun DK★★

C	Snowball	730 2	2	2	3	3	x 50gm

One colour cardigan
Rowan Rowanspun Chunky

	6	6	6	7	7	x100gm

(photographed in Fern 980)

★ Use **two strands** of Kid Classic held together throughout.
★★ Use **three strands** of Rowanspun DK held together throughout.

NEEDLES

1 pair 7mm (no 2) (US 10½) needles
1 pair 8mm (no 0) (US 11) needles

BUTTONS - 5

TENSION

12 sts and 16 rows to 10 cm measured over stocking stitch using 8mm (US 11) needles.

Fairisle cardigan

BACK
Cast on 51 (55: 59: 63: 67) sts using 7mm (US 10½) needles and yarn B.
Work in garter st for 6 rows, ending with a WS row.
Change to 8mm (US 11) needles.
Using the **fairisle** technique as described on the information page and starting and ending rows as indicated, work in patt foll chart for lower edge, which is worked entirely in st st, as folls:
Work 2 rows.
Dec 1 st at each end of next row.
49 (53: 57: 61: 65) sts.
Work rem 2 rows of lower edge chart, ending with a RS row.
Beg with a P row, cont in st st using yarn A only as folls:
Work 3 rows, ending with a WS row.
Dec 1 st at each end of next and every foll 6th row until 41 (45: 49: 53: 57) sts rem.
Work 5 rows, ending with a WS row.
Inc 1 st at each end of next and foll 6th row, then on every foll 4th row until there are 51 (55: 59: 63: 67) sts.
Work 3 rows, ending with a WS row.
Using the **fairisle** technique as described on the information page and starting and ending rows as indicated, work in patt foll chart for yoke, which is worked entirely in st st, as folls:
Work 2 rows, ending with a WS row.
Shape raglan armholes
Keeping chart correct as set until all 20 rows have been worked and then completing back in st st using yarn A, cont as folls:

Cast off 4 sts at beg of next 2 rows.
43 (47: 51: 55: 59) sts.
Dec 1 st at each end of next 1 (1: 3: 3: 5) rows, then on every foll alt row until 13 (15: 15: 17: 17) sts rem.
Work 1 row, ending with a WS row.
Cast off rem 13 (15: 15: 17: 17) sts.

LEFT FRONT
Cast on 24 (26: 28: 30: 32) sts using 7mm (US 10½) needles and yarn B.
Work in garter st for 6 rows, end with a WS row.
Change to 8mm (US 11) needles.
Starting and ending rows as indicated, work in patt foll chart for lower edge as folls:
Work 2 rows.
Dec 1 st at beg of next row.
23 (25: 27: 29: 31) sts.
Work rem 2 rows of lower edge chart, ending with a RS row.
Beg with a P row, cont in st st using yarn A only as folls: Work 3 rows, ending with a WS row.

Dec 1 st at beg of next and every foll 6th row until 19 (21: 23: 25: 27) sts rem.
Work 5 rows, ending with a WS row.
Inc 1 st at beg of next and foll 6th row, then on every foll 4th row until there are 24 (26: 28: 30: 32) sts.
Work 3 rows, ending with a WS row.
Starting and ending rows as indicated, work in patt foll chart for yoke as folls:
Work 2 rows, ending with a WS row.
Shape raglan armhole
Keeping chart correct as set until all 20 rows have been worked and then completing left front in st st using yarn A, cont as folls:
Cast off 4 sts at beg of next row.
20 (22: 24: 26: 28) sts.
Work 1 row.
Dec 1 st at raglan edge of next 1 (1: 2: 2: 2) rows.
19 (21: 22: 24: 26) sts.
Work 1 (1: 0: 0: 0) row, ending with a WS row.

(Knitting instructions continued on page 89)

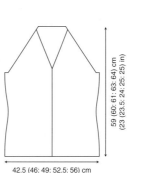
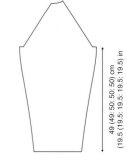

42.5 (46: 49: 52.5: 56) cm
(16.5 (18: 19.5: 20.5: 22) in)

59 (60: 61: 63: 64) cm
(23 (23.5: 24: 25: 25) in)

49 (49: 50: 50: 50) cm
(19.5 (19.5: 19.5: 19.5: 19.5) in)

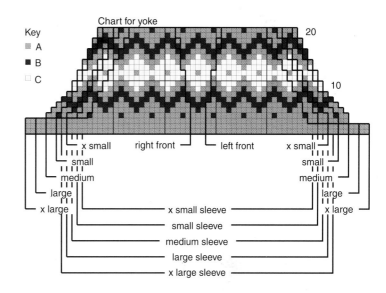

Chart for yoke

Key
▨ A
■ B
☐ C

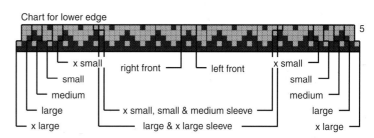

Chart for lower edge

KIRI

YARN

Rowan Kid Classic

To fit age	5-6	7-8	9-10	11-12	13-14		years
	6	7	7	8	8	x	50gm
	XS	S	M	L	XL		
To fit bust	81	86	91	97	102		cm
	32	34	36	38	40		in
	9	9	10	10	11	x	50gm

(childs photographed in Smoke 831, ladies in Royal 835)

NEEDLES

1 pair 4mm (no 8) (US 6) needles
1 pair 5mm (no 6) (US 8) needles

TENSION

19 sts and 25 rows to 10 cm measured over stocking stitch using 5mm (US 8) needles.

Pattern note: The pattern is written for the 5 childrens sizes, followed by the ladies sizes in **bold**. Where only one figure appears this applies to all sizes in that group.

BACK

Cast on 71 (77: 81: 87: 91: **97: 101: 107: 111: 117**) sts using 4mm (US 6) needles.
Work in garter st for 4 rows.
Change to 5mm (US 8) needles.
Beg with a K row, cont in st st until back measures 25 (31: 37: 42: 46: **49: 50: 50: 51: 51**) cm, ending with a WS row.

Shape armholes

Cast off 7 (**4: 4: 5: 5: 6**) sts at beg of next 2 rows.
57 (63: 67: 73: 77: **89: 93: 97: 101: 105**) sts.

Ladies sizes only

Dec 1 st at each end of next 7 rows, then on foll – (**2: 3: 4: 5: 6**) alt rows. – (**71: 73: 75: 77: 79**) sts.

All sizes

Cont straight until armhole measures 19 (20: 21: 22: 23: **21: 21: 22: 22: 23**) cm, ending with a WS row.

Shape shoulders and back neck

Cast off 4 (5: 5: 6: 7: **6**) sts at beg of next 2 rows.
49 (53: 57: 61: 63: **59: 61: 63: 65: 67**) sts.
Next row (RS): Cast off 4 (5: 5: 6: 7: **6**) sts, K until

there are 8 (9: 10: 11: 10: **9: 9: 10: 10: 11**) sts on right needle and turn, leaving rem sts on a holder.
Work each side of neck separately.
Cast off 4 sts at beg of next row.
Cast off rem 4 (5: 6: 7: 6: **5: 5: 6: 6: 7**) sts.
With RS facing, rejoin yarn to rem sts, cast off centre 25 (25: 27: 27: 29: **29: 31: 31: 33: 33**) sts, K to end. Work to match first side, reversing shapings.

FRONT

Work as given for back until 12 (12: 14: 14: 16: **18: 18: 18: 20: 20**) rows less have been worked than on back to start of shoulder shaping, ending with a WS row.

Shape neck

Next row (RS): K22 (25: 26: 29: 30: **27: 27: 28: 29: 30**) and turn, leaving rem sts on a holder.
Work each side of neck separately.
Cast off 3 (**4**) sts at beg of next row.
19 (22: 23: 26: 27: **23: 23: 24: 25: 26**) sts.
Dec 1 st at neck edge on next 5 (5: 4: 4: 3: **2**) rows, then on foll 2 (2: 3: 3: 4: **4: 4: 4: 5: 5**) alt rows.
12 (15: 16: 19: 20: **17: 17: 18: 18: 19**) sts.
Work 1 (1: 2: 2: 3: **6**) rows, ending with a WS row.

Shape shoulder

Cast off 4 (5: 5: 6: 7: **6**) sts at beg of next and foll alt row. Work 1 row.
Cast off rem 4 (5: 6: 7: 6: **5: 5: 6: 6: 7**) sts.
With RS facing, rejoin yarn to rem sts, cast off centre 13 (13: 15: 15: 17: **17: 19: 19: 19: 19**) sts, K to end. Work to match first side, reversing shapings.

SLEEVES (both alike)

Cast on 145 (153: 153: 161: 161: **169: 169: 177: 185: 185**) sts using 4mm (US 6) needles.
Row 1 (RS): K1, *K2, lift first of these 2 sts over 2nd st and off right needle, rep from * to end.
Row 2: P1, *P2tog, rep from * to end.
37 (39: 39: 41: 41: **43: 43: 45: 47: 47**) sts.
Beg with a K row, work 4 rows in st st.
Change to 5mm (US 8) needles.
Cont in st st, inc 1 st at each end of 5th and every foll 6th (**8th**) row to 41 (47: 51: 53: 47: **63: 57: 61: 63: 57**) sts, then on every foll 4th (**6th**) row until there are 73 (77: 79: 83: 87: **65: 67: 69: 71: 73**) sts.

Cont straight until sleeve measures 36 (40: 43: 45: 46: **41: 41: 42: 42: 42**) cm, ending with a WS row.

Childrens sizes only

Cast off.

Ladies sizes only

Shape top

Cast off – (**4: 4: 5: 5: 6**) sts at beg of next 2 rows. – (**57: 59: 59: 61: 61**) sts.
Dec 1 st at each end of next 3 rows, then on foll 2 alt rows, then on every foll 4th row until – (**37: 39: 37: 39: 37**) sts rem. Work 1 row.
Dec 1 st at each end of next and foll – (**0: 1: 0: 1: 0**) alt rows, then on foll 3 rows, ending with a WS row. – (**29**) sts.
Cast off 4 sts at beg of next 2 rows.
Cast off rem – (**21**) sts.

MAKING UP

PRESS all pieces as described on the info page.
Join right shoulder seam using back stitch, or mattress stitch if preferred.

Collar

With RS facing and 4mm (US 6) needles, pick up and knit 18 (18: 20: 20: 22: **23: 23: 23: 25: 25**) sts down left side of neck, 13 (13: 15: 15: 17: **17: 19: 19: 19: 19**) sts from front, 18 (18: 20: 20: 22: **23: 23: 23: 25: 25**) sts up right side of neck, then 33 (33: 35: 35: 37: **37: 39: 39: 41: 41**) sts from back.
82 (82: 90: 90: 98: **100: 104: 104: 110: 110**) sts.
Beg with a K row, work in st st for 7 (**10**) cm.
Change to 5mm (US 8) needles and cont in st st until collar measures 18 (18: 20: 20: 23: **25**) cm from pick-up row, ending with a P row.
Change to 4mm (US 6) needles.
Next row (RS of collar, WS of garment): Knit.
Next row: Purl.
Next row: *K1, M1, rep from * to last st, K1.
163 (163: 179: 179: 195: **199: 207: 207: 219: 219**) sts.
Next row: *P1, M1 purlwise, rep from * to last st, P1.
325 (325: 357: 357: 389: **397: 413: 413: 437: 437**) sts.
Cast off.

See information page for finishing instructions, setting in sleeves using the square set-in method for childrens sizes, or the set-in method for ladies sizes.

Ladies version

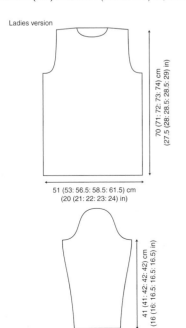

51 (53: 56.5: 58.5: 61.5) cm
(20 (21: 22: 23: 24) in)

70 (71: 72: 73: 74) cm
(27.5 (28: 28.5: 28.5: 29) in)

41 (41: 42: 42: 42) cm
(16 (16: 16.5: 16.5: 16.5) in)

Child's version

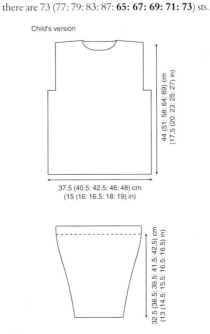

37.5 (40.5: 42.5: 46: 48) cm
(15 (16: 16.5: 18: 19) in)

44 (51: 58: 64: 69) cm
(17.5 (20: 23: 25: 27) in)

32.5 (36.5: 39.5: 41.5: 42.5) cm
(13 (14.5: 15.5: 16.5: 16.5) in)

SALEN

YARN

Rowan Felted Tweed

	XS	S	M	L	XL		
To fit bust	81	86	91	97	102	cm	
	32	34	36	38	40	in	
A Cocoa	143	5	6	6	6	7	x 50gm
B Whisper	141	2	2	2	2	2	x 50gm

NEEDLES

1 pair 3¼mm (no 10) (US 3) needles
1 pair 3¾mm (no 9) (US 5) needles

STUD FASTENERS

5

TENSION

23 sts and 32 rows to 10 cm measured over stocking stitch using 3¾mm (US 5) needles.

Pattern note: Increases for herringbone pattern (but NOT shaping) are worked as folls: place point of right needle behind left needle, insert needle point from the top down through the (purl) head of st below next st on left needle, knit this st then knit the stitch above.

BACK

Cast on 93 (99: 105: 111: 117) sts using 3¼mm (US 3) needles and yarn B.
Purl 1 row.
Now work in herringbone patt as folls:
Row 1 (RS): K4 (0: 3: 6: 2), *K2tog, K2, inc in next st (see pattern note), K2, rep from * to last 5 (1: 4: 0: 3) sts, K5 (1: 4: 0: 3).
Row 2: Purl.
Row 3: K5 (1: 4: 0: 3), *K2, inc in next st (see pattern note), K2, K2tog, rep from * to last 4 (0: 3: 6: 2) sts, K4 (0: 3: 6: 2).
Row 4: Purl.
These 4 rows form herringbone patt.
Work in herringbone patt for a further 12 rows, ending with a WS row.
Change to 3¾mm (US 5) needles.
Break off yarn B and join in yarn A.
Beg with a K row, cont in st st, shaping sides by inc 1 st at each end of 3rd and every foll 12th row until there are 105 (111: 117: 123: 129) sts.
Cont straight until back measures 27 (28: 28: 29: 29) cm, ending with a WS row.

Shape armholes

Cast off 3 (4: 4: 5: 5) sts at beg of next 2 rows. 99 (103: 109: 113: 119) sts.
Dec 1 st at each end of next 3 (3: 5: 5: 7) rows, then on foll 2 (3: 3: 4: 4) alt rows, then on foll 4th row. 87 (89: 91: 93: 95) sts.
Cont straight until armhole measures 20 (20: 21: 21: 22) cm, ending with a WS row.

Shape shoulders and back neck

Cast off 9 sts at beg of next 2 rows. 69 (71: 73: 75: 77) sts.
Next row (RS): Cast off 9 sts, K until there are 12 (12: 13: 13: 14) sts on right needle and turn, leaving rem sts on a holder.
Work each side of neck separately.
Cast off 4 sts at beg of next row.
Cast off rem 8 (8: 9: 9: 10) sts.
With RS facing, rejoin yarn to rem sts, cast off centre 27 (29: 29: 31: 31) sts, K to end.
Work to match first side, reversing shapings.

LEFT FRONT

Note: The front bands are knitted at the same time as the fronts. The front opening edge 8 sts will be folded to the WS and the finished front edge is marked by the slipped stitch.
Cast on 63 (66: 69: 72: 75) sts using 3¼mm (US 3) needles and yarn B.
Purl 1 row.
Now work in herringbone patt as folls:
Row 1 (RS): K4 (0: 3: 6: 2), *K2tog, K2, inc in next st (see pattern note), K2, rep from * to last 10 sts, K1, sl 1 purlwise, K8.
Row 2: Purl.
Row 3: K5 (1: 4: 0: 3), *K2, inc in next st (see pattern note), K2, K2tog, rep from * to last 9 sts, sl 1 purlwise, K8.
Row 4:
These 4 rows set the sts - herringbone patt with front edge 8 sts in st st.
Cont as set for a further 12 rows, ending with a WS row.
Change to 3¾mm (US 5) needles.
Join in yarn A.
Next row (RS): Using yarn A K46 (49: 52: 55: 58), using yarn B patt 17 sts.
Next row: Using yarn B patt 17 sts, using yarn A P46 (49: 52: 55: 58).
These 2 rows set the sts – front opening edge 17 sts worked as before using yarn B with all other sts now worked in st st using yarn A.
Keeping sts correct as set, inc 1 st at beg of next and every foll 12th row until there are 69 (72: 75: 78: 81) sts.
Cont straight until left front matches back to beg of armhole shaping, ending with a WS row.

Shape armhole

Cast off 3 (4: 4: 5: 5) sts at beg of next row. 66 (68: 71: 73: 76) sts.
Work 1 row.
Dec 1 st at armhole edge of next 3 (3: 5: 5: 7) rows, then on foll 2 (3: 3: 4: 4) alt rows, then on foll 4th row. 60 (61: 62: 63: 64) sts.
Cont straight until 23 (23: 23: 25: 25) rows less have been worked than on back to start of shoulder shaping, ending with a RS row.

Shape neck

Next row (WS): Patt 24 (25: 25: 25: 25) sts and slip these sts onto a holder for neckband, P to end. 36 (36: 37: 38: 39) sts.
Dec 1 st at neck edge of next 5 rows, then on foll 4 (4: 4: 5: 5) alt rows, then on foll 4th row. 26 (26: 27: 27: 28) sts.
Work 5 rows, ending with a WS row.

Shape shoulder

Cast off 9 sts at beg of next and foll alt row.
Work 1 row. Cast off rem 8 (8: 9: 9: 10) sts.

RIGHT FRONT

Cast on 63 (66: 69: 72: 75) sts using 3¼mm (US 3) needles and yarn B.
Purl 1 row.
Now work in herringbone patt as folls:
Row 1 (RS): K8, sl 1 purlwise, *K2tog, K2, inc in next st (see pattern note), K2, rep from * to last 5 (1: 4: 0: 3) sts, K5 (1: 4: 0: 3).
Row 2: Purl.
Row 3: K8, sl 1 purlwise, K1, *K2, inc in next st (see pattern note), K2, K2tog, rep from * to last 4 (0: 3: 6: 2) sts, K4 (0: 3: 6: 2).

Row 4: Purl.
These 4 rows set the sts - herringbone patt with front edge 8 sts in st st.
Cont as set for a further 12 rows, ending with a WS row.
Change to 3¾mm (US 5) needles.
Join in yarn A.
Next row (RS): Using yarn B patt 17 sts, using yarn A K46 (49: 52: 55: 58).
Next row: Using yarn A P46 (49: 52: 55: 58), using yarn B patt 17 sts.
These 2 rows set the sts – front opening edge 17 sts worked as before using yarn B with all other sts now worked in st st using yarn A.
Keeping sts correct as set, inc 1 st at end of next and every foll 12th row until there are 69 (72: 75: 78: 81) sts.
Complete to match left front, reversing shapings.

SLEEVES (both alike)

Cast on 50 (50: 52: 54: 54) sts using 3¼mm (US 3) needles and yarn B.
Purl 1 row.
Now work in herringbone patt as folls:
Row 1 (RS): K0 (0: 1: 2: 2), *K2tog, K2, inc in next st (see pattern note), K2, rep from * to last 1 (1: 2: 3: 3) sts, K1 (1: 2: 3: 3).
Row 2: Purl.
Row 3: K1 (1: 2: 3: 3), *K2, inc in next st (see pattern note), K2, K2tog, rep from * to last 0 (0: 1: 2: 2) sts, K0 (0: 1: 2: 2).
Row 4: Purl.
These 4 rows form herringbone patt.
Work in herringbone patt for a further 12 rows, ending with a WS row.
Change to 3¾mm (US 5) needles.
Break off yarn B and join in yarn A.
Beg with a K row, cont in st st, shaping sides by inc 1 st at each end of 3rd and every foll 10th (8th: 8th: 8th: 8th) row to 58 (78: 80: 82: 78) sts, then on every foll 8th (-: -: -: 6th) row until there are 76 (-: -: -: 84) sts.
Cont straight until sleeve measures 43 (43: 44: 44: 44) cm, ending with a WS row.

(Knitting instructions continued on page 88)

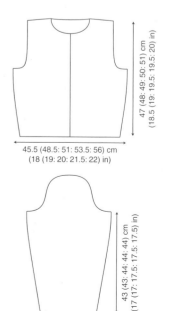

45.5 (48.5: 51: 53.5: 56) cm
(18 (19: 20: 21.5: 22) in)

47 (48: 49: 50: 51) cm
(18.5 (19.5: 19.5: 19.5: 20) in)

43 (43: 44: 44: 44) cm
(17 (17: 17.5: 17.5: 17.5) in)

CHARLOTTE

YARN

Rowan Kid Classic

	XS	S	M	L	XL	
To fit bust	81	86	91	97	102	cm
	32	34	36	38	40	in
Scoop neck	5	5	5	6	6	x 50gm
Single polo neck	5	6	6	7	7	x 50gm

(scoop neck sweater photographed in Bewitch 830, single polo neck sweater in Cherish 833)

NEEDLES

1 pair 4½mm (no 7) (US 7) needles
1 pair 5mm (no 6) (US 8) needles

TENSION

19 sts and 25 rows to 10 cm measured over stocking stitch using 5mm (US 8) needles.

Scoop neck sweater

BACK

Using 4½mm (US 7) needles, cast on 69 (73: 79: 83: 89) sts.
Row 1 (RS): P3 (2: 2: 1: 1), *K3, P3, rep from * to last 6 (5: 5: 4: 4) sts, K3, P3 (2: 2: 1: 1).
Row 2: K3 (2: 2: 1: 1), *P3, K3, rep from * to last 6 (5: 5: 4: 4) sts, P3, K3 (2: 2: 1: 1).
Rep last 2 rows 9 times more.
Change to 5mm (US 8) needles.
Beg with a K row, cont in st st as folls:
Work 2 rows.
Next row (RS): K2, M1, K to last 2 sts, M1, K2.
Working all increases as set by last row, inc 1 st at each end of every foll 10th row until there are 77 (81: 87: 91: 97) sts.
Cont straight until back measures 25 (26: 26: 27: 27) cm, ending with a WS row.
Shape armholes
Cast off 3 (4: 4: 5: 5) sts at beg of next 2 rows.
71 (73: 79: 81: 87) sts.
Dec 1 st at each end of next 3 (3: 5: 5: 7) rows, then on foll 3 alt rows.
59 (61: 63: 65: 67) sts.★★
Cont straight until armhole measures 10 (10: 11: 11: 12) cm, ending with a WS row.
Shape back neck
Next row (RS): K19 (19: 20: 20: 21) and turn, leaving rem sts on a holder.
Work each side of neck separately.
Cast off 4 sts at beg of next and foll alt row.
11 (11: 12: 12: 13) sts.
Dec 1 st at neck edge of next 3 rows, then on foll 4 alt rows, then on foll 4th row. 3 (3: 4: 4: 5) sts.
Work 3 rows, ending with a WS row.
Shape shoulder
Cast off.
With RS facing, rejoin yarn to rem sts, cast off centre 21 (23: 23: 25: 25) sts, K to end.
Work to match first side, reversing shapings.

FRONT

Work as given for back until 6 rows less have been worked than on back to start of back neck shaping, ending with a WS row.
Shape front neck
Next row (RS): K19 (19: 20: 20: 21) and turn, leaving rem sts on a holder.
Work each side of neck separately.
Cast off 4 sts at beg of next and foll alt row.
11 (11: 12: 12: 13) sts.

Dec 1 st at neck edge of next 3 rows, then on foll 2 alt rows, then on every foll 4th row until 3 (3: 4: 4: 5) sts rem. Work 5 rows, ending with a WS row.
Shape shoulder
Cast off.
With RS facing, rejoin yarn to rem sts, cast off centre 21 (23: 23: 25: 25) sts, K to end.
Work to match first side, reversing shapings.

SLEEVES

Using 4½mm (US 7) needles, cast on 43 (43: 45: 47: 47) sts.
Row 1 (RS): K2 (2: 3: 1: 1), *P3, K3, rep from * to last 5 (5: 6: 4: 4) sts, P3, K2 (2: 3: 1: 1).
Row 2: P2 (2: 3: 1: 1), *K3, P3, rep from * to last 5 (5: 6: 4: 4) sts, K3, P2 (2: 3: 1: 1).
Rep last 2 rows 9 times more, inc 1 st at each end of 11th of these rows. 45 (45: 47: 49: 49) sts.
Change to 5mm (US 8) needles.
Beg with a K row, cont in st st as folls:
Work 4 (2: 2: 2: 2) rows.
Next row (RS): K2, M1, K to last 2 sts, M1, K2.
Working all increases as set by last row, inc 1 st at each end of every foll 12th (10th: 10th: 10th: 10th) row to 49 (57: 61: 63: 55) sts, then on every foll 10th (8th: 8th: 8th: 8th) row until there are 61 (63: 65: 67: 69) sts.
Cont straight until sleeve measures 43 (43: 44: 44: 44) cm, ending with a WS row.
Shape top
Cast off 3 (4: 4: 5: 5) sts at beg of next 2 rows. 55 (55: 57: 57: 59) sts.
Dec 1 st at each end of next 3 rows, then on every foll alt row until 33 sts rem.
Dec 1 st at each end of next 3 rows, ending with a WS row. 27 sts. Cast off 4 sts at beg of next 2 rows.
Cast off rem 19 sts.

Single polo neck sweater

BACK

Work as given for back of scoop neck sweater to ★★.
Cont straight until armhole measures 19 (19: 20: 20: 21) cm, ending with a WS row.
Shape shoulders and back neck
Cast off 5 sts at beg of next 2 rows.
49 (51: 53: 55: 57) sts.
Next row (RS): Cast off 5 sts, K until there are 8 (8: 9: 9: 10) sts on right needle and turn, leaving rem sts on a holder.
Work each side of neck separately.
Cast off 4 sts at beg of next row.
Cast off rem 4 (4: 5: 5: 6) sts.
With RS facing, rejoin yarn to rem sts, cast off centre 23 (25: 25: 27: 27) sts, K to end.
Work to match first side, reversing shapings.

FRONT

Work as given for back until 18 (18: 18: 20: 20) rows less have been worked than on back to start of shoulder shaping, ending with a WS row.
Shape neck
Next row (RS): K21 (21: 22: 23: 24) and turn, leaving rem sts on a holder.
Work each side of neck separately.
Dec 1 st at neck edge of next 4 rows, then on foll 2 (2: 2: 3: 3) alt rows, then on foll 4th row.
14 (14: 15: 15: 16) sts.
Work 5 rows, ending with a WS row.

Shape shoulder
Cast off 5 sts at beg of next and foll alt row.
Work 1 row.
Cast off rem 4 (4: 5: 5: 6) sts.
With RS facing, rejoin yarn to rem sts, cast off centre 17 (19: 19: 19: 19) sts, K to end.
Work to match first side, reversing shapings.

SLEEVES

Work as given for sleeves of scoop neck sweater.

MAKING UP

PRESS all pieces as described on the info page.
Join right shoulder seam using back stitch, or mattress stitch if preferred.
Scoop neck sweater
Neckband
With RS facing and using 4½mm (US 7) needles, pick up and knit 32 sts down left side of front neck, 21 (23: 23: 25: 25) sts from front, 32 sts up right side of front neck, 26 (27: 27: 28: 28) sts down right side of back neck, 21 (23: 23: 25: 25) sts from back, and 26 (27: 27: 28: 28) sts up left side of back neck. 158 (164: 164: 170: 170) sts.
Row 1 (WS): K1, *K3, P3, rep from * to last st, K1.
Rep this row 11 times more.
Cast off in rib.
Single polo neck sweater
Collar
With RS facing and using 4½mm (US 7) needles, pick up and knit 22 (22: 22: 25: 25) sts down left side of neck, 17 (19: 19: 19: 19) sts from front, 22 (22: 22: 25: 25) sts up right side of neck, then 31 (33: 33: 35: 35) sts from back.
92 (96: 96: 104: 104) sts.
Row 1 (WS): *K2, P2, rep from * to end.
Rep this row until collar measures 10 cm.
Cast off in rib.
Both sweaters
See information page for finishing instructions, setting in sleeves using the set-in method.

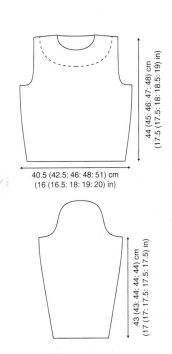

40.5 (42.5: 46: 48: 51) cm
(16 (16.5: 18: 19: 20) in)

44 (45: 46: 47: 48) cm
(17.5 (17.5: 18: 18.5: 19) in)

43 (43: 44: 44: 44) cm
(17 (17: 17.5: 17.5: 17.5) in)

FIN BERET

YARN
Rowan Kidsilk Haze
Multi colour version

A Liqueur	595	1	x	25gm
B Toffee	598	1	x	25gm
C Marmalade	596	1	x	25gm
D Lord	593	1	x	25gm
E Heavenly	592	1	x	25gm
F Jelly	597	1	x	25gm
One colour version		2	x	25gm

(not photographed)
Use **3 strands** of yarn held together throughout.

NEEDLES
1 pair 3¾mm (no 9) (US 5) needles
1 pair 4½mm (no 7) (US 7) needles

TENSION
19 sts and 25 rows to 10 cm measured over stocking stitch using 4½mm (US 7) needles and **3 strands of yarn** held together.

MEASUREMENTS
To fit average size ladies head.

Opposite: Charlotte Scoop Neck Sweater knitted in Kid Classic, knitting instructions on page 75

Multi Colour Beret
Cast on 84 sts using 3¾mm (US 5) needles and yarn A.
Join in yarn B.
Row 1 (RS): Using yarn B, ★K2, P2, rep from ★ to end.
Rep last row 7 times more, inc 1 st at end of last row. 85 sts.
Next row (RS): Using yarn A, (K3, M1) 28 times, K1. 113 sts.
Change to 5mm (US 8) needles.
Beg with a P row and joining in and breaking off colours as required, cont in st st as folls:
Using yarn A, work 1 row.
Using yarn C, work 1 row.
Using yarn A, work 1 row.
Using yarn B, work 2 rows.
Using yarn D, work 2 rows.
Using yarn E, work 1 row.
Using yarn C, work 1 row.

Shape top
Row 1 (RS): Using yarn C, (K8, M1) 14 times, K1. 127 sts.
Using yarn A, work 4 rows.
Using yarn B, work 2 rows.
Using yarn F, work 1 row.
Using yarn A, work 1 row.
Using yarn D, work 1 row.
Using yarn E, work 2 rows.
Row 13 (RS): Using yarn C, (K7, K2tog) 14 times, K1. 113 sts.

Using yarn D, work 1 row.
Using yarn F, work 1 row.
Using yarn B, work 1 row.
Row 17 (RS): Using yarn C, (K13, K3tog) 7 times, K1. 99 sts.
Using yarn C, work 2 rows.
Using yarn F, work 1 row.
Row 21 (RS): Using yarn F, (K11, K3tog) 7 times, K1. 85 sts.
Using yarn B, work 2 rows.
Using yarn E, work 1 row.
Row 25 (RS): Using yarn B, (K9, K3tog) 7 times, K1. 71 sts.
Using yarn A, work 1 row.
Using yarn C, work 1 row.
Using yarn D, work 1 row.
Row 29 (RS): Using yarn D, (K7, K3tog) 7 times, K1. 57 sts.
Cont using yarn B only as folls:
Work 1 row.
Row 31 (RS): (K5, K3tog) 7 times, K1. 43 sts.
Row 32: P1, (P3tog, P3) 7 times, K1. 29 sts.
Row 33: (K1, K3tog) 7 times, K1.
Break yarn and thread through rem 15 sts.
Pull up tight and fasten off securely.
Sew back seam using back stitch.

One Colour Beret
Work as for multi colour beret but using one colour throughout.

BAY BERET

YARN
Rowan Lurex Shimmer
To fit average sized adult head

2	x	25gm

(photographed in Black 334)

NEEDLES
1 pair 3¼mm (no 10) (US 3) needles
1 pair 4mm (no 8) (US 6) needles

TENSION
22 sts and 30 rows to 10 cm measured over stocking stitch using 4mm (US 6) needles.

Beret
Cast on 91 sts using 3¼mm (US 3) needles.
Row 1 (RS): K1, ★P1, K1, rep from ★ to end.
Row 2: P1, ★K1, P1, rep from ★ to end.
Rep these 2 rows for 2.5 cm, ending with a WS row.
Next row (RS): ★K3, M1, K4, M1, rep from ★ to last st, K1. 127 sts.
Change to 4mm (US 6) needles.
Beg with a P row, cont in st st as folls:
Work 11 rows, ending with a WS row.
Next row (RS): ★K9, M1, rep from ★ to last st, K1. 141 sts.
Work 13 rows, ending with a WS row.

Shape top
Row 1 (RS): ★K8, K2tog, rep from ★ to last st, K1. 127 sts.
Work 7 rows.
Row 9: ★K15, K3tog, rep from ★ to last st, K1. 113 sts.
Work 3 rows.
Row 13: ★K13, K3tog, rep from ★ to last st, K1. 99 sts.
Work 3 rows.
Row 17: ★K11, K3tog, rep from ★ to last st, K1. 85 sts.
Work 3 rows.
Row 21: ★K9, K3tog, rep from ★ to last st, K1. 71 sts.
Work 1 row.
Row 23: ★K7, K3tog, rep from ★ to last st, K1. 57 sts.
Work 1 row.
Row 25: ★K5, K3tog, rep from ★ to last st, K1. 43 sts.
Work 1 row.
Row 27: ★K3, K3tog, rep from ★ to last st, K1. 29 sts.
Row 28: P1, ★P3tog, P1, rep from ★ to end. 15 sts.
Break yarn and thread through rem 15 sts. Pull up tight and fasten off securely.

MAKING UP
PRESS as described on the information page.
Join back seam.

ROSE

YARN

Kidsilk Haze and Lurex Shimmer

	XS	S	M	L	XL	
To fit bust	81	86	91	97	102 cm
	32	34	36	38	40 in

Polo neck vest

Kidsilk Haze	3	3	3	4	4 x 25gm
(photographed in Heavenly 592)					

V neck vest

Kidsilk Haze and Lurex Shimmer

Kidsilk Haze						
A Marmalade 596	2	3	3	3	3 x 25gm
Lurex Shimmer						
B Ant Gold 332	1	1	1	1	1 x 25gm

Slash neck vest

Kidsilk Haze						
A Pearl	590	2	3	3	3	3 x 25gm
B Wicked	599	1	1	1	1	1 x 25gm

NEEDLES

1 pair 3mm (no 11) (US 2/3) needles
1 pair 3¼mm (no 10) (US 3) needles
Polo neck vest only: 1 3mm (no 11) (US 2/3)
circular needle

BEADS (optional) – polo neck vest only:

approx 750 beads

TENSION

25 sts and 34 rows to 10 cm measured over
stocking stitch using 3¼mm (US 3) needles.

Polo neck vest

Beading note: Beads are optional.
If using beads, thread them onto yarn before
beginning, threading approx 250 beads onto first
ball. Place beads within knitting as folls: bring
yarn to front (RS) of work and slip next st
purlwise, slide bead along yarn so that it sits in
front of st just slipped, then take yarn to back
(WS) of work.
For unbeaded version, work as given for beaded
version replacing "bead 1" with "K1".

BACK
Cast on 95 (101: 107: 113: 119) sts using 3mm
(US 2/3) needles.
Beg with a P row, work in rev st st for 6 rows.
Place markers at ends of last row.
Now cont in bead patt as folls:
Beg with a K row, work in st st for 4 rows.
Row 5 (RS): K2, ★place bead (see beading
note), K5, rep from ★ to last 3 sts, place bead, K2.
Beg with a P row, work 5 rows in st st.
Change to 3¼mm (US 3) needles.
Work in st st for a further 2 rows, shaping side
seams by dec 1 st at each end of first of these rows.
93 (99: 105: 111: 117) sts.

Row 13 (RS): K4, ★place bead (see beading
note), K5, rep from ★ to last 5 sts, place bead, K4.
Beg with a P row, work 3 rows in st st.
These 16 rows set bead patt and begin side seam
shaping.
Cont in patt, dec 1 st at each end of 3rd and foll
8th row.
89 (95: 101: 107: 113) sts.
Work 13 (15: 15: 15: 15) rows, ending with a WS row.
Inc 1 st at each end of next and every foll 10th
row until there are 101 (107: 113: 119: 125) sts,
taking inc sts into patt.
Cont straight until back measures 29 (30: 30: 31:
31) cm **from markers**, ending with a WS row.
Shape armholes
Keeping patt correct, cast off 4 (4: 5: 5: 6) sts at beg
of next 2 rows, then 4 sts at beg of foll 2 rows.
85 (91: 95: 101: 105) sts.
Dec 1 st at each end of next 3 (5: 5: 7: 7) rows,
then on foll 4 (4: 5: 5: 6) alt rows.
71 (73: 75: 77: 79) sts.
Cont straight until armhole measures 20 (20: 21:
21: 22) cm, ending with a WS row.
Shape shoulders and back neck
Cast off 4 (4: 4: 4: 5) sts at beg of next 2 rows.
63 (65: 67: 69: 69) sts.
Next row (RS): Cast off 4 (4: 4: 4: 5) sts, patt
until there are 8 (8: 9: 9: 8) sts on right needle and
turn, leaving rem sts on a holder.
Work each side of neck separately.
Cast off 4 sts at beg of next row.
Cast off rem 4 (4: 5: 5: 4) sts.
With RS facing, rejoin yarn to rem sts, cast off
centre 39 (41: 41: 43: 43) sts, patt to end.
Work to match first side, reversing shapings.

FRONT
Work as given for back until 26 (26: 26: 28: 28) rows
less have been worked before start of shoulder
shaping, ending with a WS row.
Shape neck
Next row (RS): Patt 25 (25: 26: 27: 28) sts and
turn, leaving rem sts on a holder.
Work each side of neck separately.
Cast off 5 sts at beg of next row.
20 (20: 21: 22: 23) sts.
Dec 1 st at neck edge on next 3 rows, then on foll
3 (3: 3: 4: 4) alt rows, then on every foll 4th row
until 12 (12: 13: 13: 14) sts rem.
Work 7 rows, ending with a WS row.
Shape shoulder
Cast off 4 (4: 4: 4: 5) sts at beg of next and foll alt row.
Work 1 row.
Cast off rem 4 (4: 5: 5: 4) sts.
With RS facing, rejoin yarn to rem sts, cast off
centre 21 (23: 23: 23: 23) sts, patt to end.
Work to match first side, reversing shapings.

V neck vest
BACK
Cast on 95 (101: 107: 113: 119) sts using 3mm
(US 2/3) needles and yarn A.
Beg with a P row, work in rev st st for 6 rows.
Beg with a K row, work in st st for 8 (10: 10: 10:
10) rows.
Change to 3¼mm (US 3) needles.
Extra small size only
Work 2 rows, dec 1 st at each end of first of these
rows. 93 sts.

All sizes
Join in yarn B and cont in st st in stripe patt as
folls:
Using yarn B, work 1 row, dec 0 (1: 1: 0: 0) st at
each end of row. 93 (99: 105: 113: 119) sts.
Using yarn A and beg with a P row, work 11 rows,
dec 1 st at each end of 6th (8th: 8th: 2nd: 2nd)
and foll – (-: -: 8th: 8th) row.
91 (97: 103: 109: 115) sts.
These 12 rows form stripe patt and begin side
seam shaping.
Cont in striped st st as set, dec 1 st at each end of
8th row from previous dec.
89 (95: 101: 107: 113) sts.
Work 13 (15: 15: 17: 17) rows, ending with a WS
row.★★
Inc 1 st at each end of next and every foll 10th
row until there are 101 (107: 113: 119: 125) sts.
Work 9 rows, ending with a WS row.
Shape armholes
Cast off 4 (4: 5: 5: 6) sts at beg of next 2 rows, then
4 sts at beg of foll 2 rows. 85 (91: 95: 101: 105) sts.
Dec 1 st at each end of next 3 (5: 5: 7: 7) rows,
then on foll 4 (4: 5: 5: 6) alt rows.
71 (73: 75: 77: 79) sts.
Cont straight until armhole measures 20 (20: 21:
21: 22) cm, ending with a WS row.
Shape shoulders and back neck
Cast off 7 (7: 7: 7: 8) sts at beg of next 2 rows.
57 (59: 61: 63: 63) sts.
Next row (RS): Cast off 7 (7: 7: 7: 8) sts, K until
there are 11 (11: 12: 12: 11) sts on right needle and
turn, leaving rem sts on a holder.
Work each side of neck separately.
Cast off 4 sts at beg of next row.
Cast off rem 7 (7: 8: 8: 7) sts.
With RS facing, rejoin yarn to rem sts, cast off
centre 21 (23: 23: 25: 25) sts, K to end.
Work to match first side, reversing shapings.

(Knitting instructions continued on page 80)

49 (50: 51: 52: 53) cm
(19.5 (19.5: 20: 20.5: 21) in)

40.5 (43: 45: 47.5: 50) cm
(16 (17: 17.5: 18.5: 19.5) in)

*Opposite: Rose V Neck Vest knitted in
Kidsilk Haze & Lurex Shimmer & Katie
Jacket knitted in Rowanspun DK, knitting
instructions on page 39*

ROSE

Continued from page 79

FRONT

Work as given for back to **.
Inc 1 st at each end of next and every foll 10th row until there are 97 (103: 109: 115: 121) sts.
Work 3 rows, ending with a WS row.
Shape neck
Next row (RS): K48 (51: 54: 57: 60) and turn, leaving rem sts on a holder.
Work each side of neck separately.
Work 5 rows.
Inc 1 st at beg (side seam edge) of next and foll 10th row **and at same time** dec 1 st at end (neck edge) of 3rd and foll 8th row.
48 (51: 54: 57: 60) sts.
Work 7 rows.
Dec 1 st at neck edge of next row.
47 (50: 53: 56: 59) sts.
Work 1 row, ending with a WS row. (Front now matches back to beg of armhole shaping.)
Shape armhole
Cast off 4 (4: 5: 5: 6) sts at beg of next row, then 4 sts at beg of foll alt row.
39 (42: 44: 47: 49) sts.
Work 1 row.
Dec 1 st at armhole edge of next 3 (5: 5: 7: 7) rows, then on foll 4 (4: 5: 5: 6) alt rows **and at same time** dec 1 st at neck edge of next and every foll 6th row.
30 (30: 31: 32: 32) sts.
Dec 1 st at neck edge only on every foll 6th row from previous dec until 23 (26: 26: 29: 28) sts rem, then on every foll 4th row until 21 (21: 22: 22: 23) sts rem.
Cont straight until front matches back to start of shoulder shaping, ending with a WS row.
Shape shoulder
Cast off 7 (7: 7: 7: 8) sts at beg of next and foll alt row.
Work 1 row.
Cast off rem 7 (7: 8: 8: 7) sts.

With RS facing, rejoin yarn to rem sts, K2tog, K to end.
Work to match first side, reversing shapings.

Slash neck vest
BACK and FRONT (both alike)
Cast on 95 (101: 107: 113: 119) sts using 3mm (US 2/3) needles and yarn A.
Beg with a P row, work in rev st st for 6 rows.
Place markers at both ends of last row.
Beg with a K row, cont in st st as folls:
Work 10 rows.
Change to 3¼mm (US 3) needles.
Work a further 2 rows, dec 1 st at each end of first of these rows.
93 (99: 105: 111: 117) sts.
Join in yarn B and cont in st st in stripe patt as folls:
Using yarn B, work 1 row.
Using yarn A and beg with a P row, work 15 rows, dec 1 st at each end of every foll 8th row from previous dec.
89 (95: 101: 107: 113) sts.
These 16 rows form stripe patt and begin side seam shaping.
Work a further 12 (14: 14: 14: 14) rows, ending with a WS row.
Inc 1 st at each end of next and every foll 10th row until there are 101 (107: 113: 119: 125) sts.
Cont straight until work measures 29 (30: 30: 31: 31) cm **from markers**, ending with a WS row.
Shape armholes
Cast off 4 (4: 5: 5: 6) sts at beg of next 2 rows, then 4 sts at beg of foll 2 rows.
85 (91: 95: 101: 105) sts.
Dec 1 st at each end of next 3 (5: 5: 7: 7) rows, then on foll 4 (4: 5: 5: 6) alt rows.
71 (73: 75: 77: 79) sts.
Cont straight until armhole measures 17.5 (17.5: 18.5: 18.5: 19.5) cm, ending with a WS row.
Shape neck
Next row (RS): K15 (15: 16: 16: 17) and turn, leaving rem sts on a holder.
Work each side of neck separately.
Cast off 5 sts at beg of next row.
10 (10: 11: 11: 12) sts.
Dec 1 st at neck edge of next 3 rows, then on foll alt row.
6 (6: 7: 7: 8) sts.
Work 1 row, ending with a WS row.
Shape shoulder
Cast off rem 6 (6: 7: 7: 8) sts.
With RS facing, rejoin yarn to rem sts, cast off centre 41 (43: 43: 45: 45) sts, K to end.
Work to match first side, reversing shapings.

MAKING UP
PRESS all pieces as described on the info page.
Join right shoulder seam using back stitch, or mattress stitch if preferred.
Polo neck vest
Collar
With RS facing and 3mm (US 2/3) needles, pick up and knit 33 (33: 33: 35: 35) sts down left side of neck, 21 (23: 23: 23: 23) sts from front, 33 (33: 33: 35: 35) sts up right side of neck, then 46 (50: 50: 52: 52) sts from back.
133 (139: 139: 145: 145) sts.
Beg with a K row, work in st st for 26 rows.

Break yarn, thread beads onto yarn and then rejoin yarn.
Next row (RS): K2, *place bead, K5, rep from * to last 5 sts, place bead, K4.
Work in st st for a further 7 rows.
Next row: *K5, place bead, rep from * to last st, K1.
Work in st st for a further 7 rows.
Last 16 rows form bead patt.
Cont in patt until collar measures 10 cm.
Change to 3¼mm (US 3) needles and cont in patt until collar measures 25 cm, ending with a purl row.
Work edging
Change to 3mm (US 2/3) circular needle.
Work in st st for a further 2 rows.
Next row (RS): *K1, M1, rep from * to last st, K1. 265 (277: 277: 289: 289) sts.
Next row: Purl.
Rep last 2 rows once more.
529 (553: 553: 577: 577) sts.
Cast off knitwise.
V neck vest
Neckband
With RS facing, 3mm (US 2/3) needles and yarn A, pick up and knit 75 (75: 78: 78: 80) sts down left side of neck, 75 (75: 78: 78: 80) sts up right side of neck, then 29 (31: 31: 33: 33) sts from back. 179 (181: 187: 189: 193) sts.
Cast off knitwise (on WS).
Slash neck vest
Neckband
With RS facing, 3mm (US 2/3) needles and yarn A, pick up and knit 12 sts down left side of front neck, 41 (43: 43: 45: 45) sts from front, 12 sts up right side of front neck, 12 sts down right side of back neck, 41 (43: 43: 45: 45) sts from back, then 12 sts up left side of back neck.
130 (134: 134: 138: 138) sts.
Beg with a K row, work in rev st st for 6 rows.
Cast off knitwise (on WS).
All vests
Join left shoulder and collar/neckband seam using back stitch, or mattress stitch if preferred, reversing seam for turn-back of polo neck vest.
Armhole borders (both alike)
With RS facing and 3mm (US 2/3) needles (and using yarn A for polo and slash neck vests), pick up and knit 120 (120: 127: 127: 134) sts evenly around armhole edge.
Cast off knitwise (on WS).
See information page for finishing instructions.

Rose Polo Neck Vest knitted in Kidsilk Haze, knitting instructions on page 79 & Spencer Sweater knitted in Rowanspun DK, knitting instructions on page 49

RUTH

Continued from page 4

MAKING UP
PRESS all pieces as described on the
information page.
Join shoulder seams using back stitch, or mattress
stitch if preferred.

Neckband
With RS facing and 3¾mm (US 5) needles, pick
up and knit 39 sts up right side of neck, 35 sts
from back, then 39 sts down left side of neck.
113 sts.
Cast off knitwise (on WS).
See information page for finishing instructions,
setting in sleeves using the set-in method and
attaching stud fasteners to front opening edges
so that they overlap by 16 sts.

58 cm (23 in)

45 cm (17.5 in)

43 cm (17 in)

Body chart

Key
K on RS,
P on WS
K2tog
inc

186
180
170
160
150
140
130
122
110
100
90
80
70
60
50
40
30
20
10

Back

Left front
Right front

Back

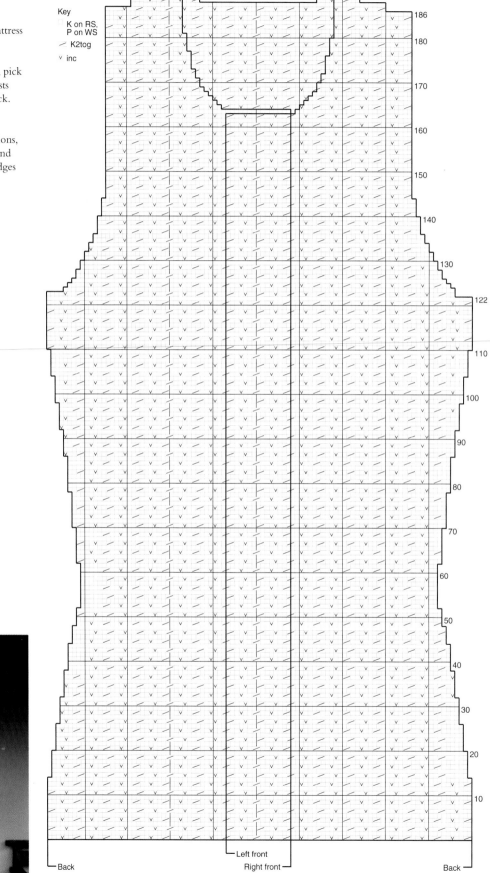

HAMISH

Continued from page 11

Row 1 (WS): ★K4, P2, rep from ★ to end.
Row 2: ★K2, P4, rep from ★ to end.
Rep these 2 rows for 6 (**7**: 8) cm.
Change to 8mm (US 11) needles and cont in rib
as set until collar measures 16 (**18**: 20) cm from
pick-up row. Cast off in rib.

Shawl neck sweater

Join shoulder seams using back stitch, or mattress
stitch if preferred.

Collar

Cast on 64 (64: 70: 70: 70: **76**: 82) sts using 7mm
(US 10½) needles.
Row 1 (RS): K4, ★P2, K4, rep from ★ to end.
Row 2: P4, ★K2, P4, rep from ★ to end.
Rep last 2 rows for 16.5 (16.5: 18: 18: 18: **20**: 21.5) cm.
Cast off in rib.
Overlapping ends of collar, sew collar to neck
edge, matching collar cast-on edge to front row
end edges and back neck, and collar row end
edges to front cast-off sts.

Both sweaters

See information page for finishing instructions,
setting in sleeves using the square set-in method
for childrens sizes, or the shallow set-in method
for ladies and mens sizes.

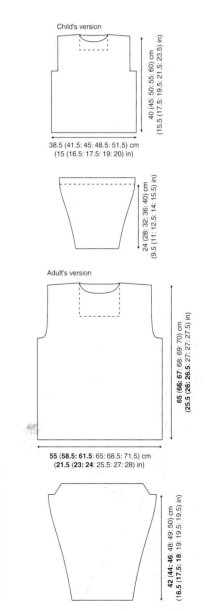

Child's version

40 (45: 50: 55: 60) cm
(15.5 (17.5: 19.5: 21.5: 23.5) in)

38.5 (41.5: 45: 48.5: 51.5) cm
(15 (16.5: 17.5: 19: 20) in)

24 (28: 32: 36: 40) cm
(9.5 (11: 12.5: 14: 15.5) in)

Adult's version

65 (**66**: 67: 68: 69: 70) cm
(25.5 (**26**: 26.5: 27: 27: 27.5) in)

55 (**58.5**: 61.5: 65: 68.5: 71.5) cm
(21.5 (**23**: 24: 25.5: 27: 28) in)

42 (**44**: 46: 48: 49: 50) cm
(16.5 (**17.5**: 18: 19: 19.5: 19.5) in)

Sleeve chart

178
170
160
150
138
130
120
110
100
90
80
70
60
50
40
30
20
10

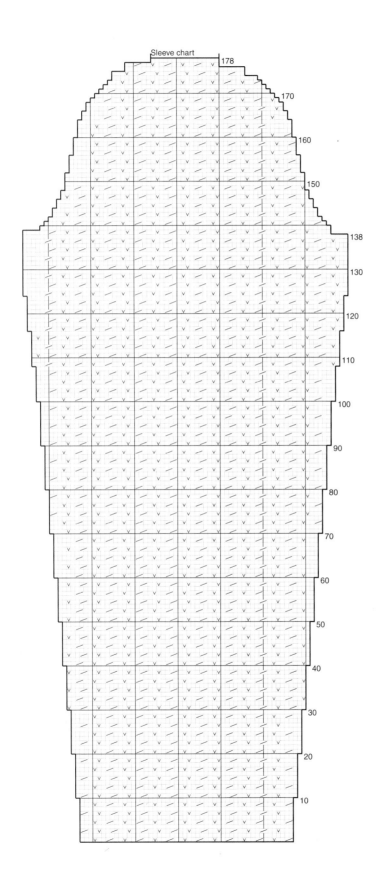

CAMERON

Continued from page 8

Beg with a **purl** row, cont in st st, shaping sides by inc 1 st at each end of 4th and every foll 6th row to 53 (53: 67: 71: 69: **79: 77: 69:** 79: 71: 65) sts, then on every foll 4th row until there are 63 (67: 71: 73: 77: **81: 83: 87:** 89: 93: 97) sts.
Cont straight until sleeve measures 29 (33: 37: 41: 43: **46: 47: 47:** 49: 49: 50) cm, end with a WS row.

Shape top
Cast off 4 sts at beg of next 2 rows.
55 (59: 63: 65: 69: **73: 75: 79:** 81: 85: 89) sts.

Childrens sizes only
Work 6 rows, dec 1 st at each end of 3rd of these rows.

Ladies and mens sizes only
Dec 1 st at each end of next and foll 4 alt rows.
Work 1 row, ending with a WS row.

All sizes
Cast off rem 53 (57: 61: 63: 67: **63: 65: 69:** 71: 75: 79) sts.

Crew neck sweater
BACK
Work as given for **front** of laced neck sweater to ★★.
Working in trellis patt throughout, cont straight until armhole measures 20 (21: 22: 23: 24: **25: 26: 27:** 28: 29: 30) cm, ending with a WS row.

Shape shoulders and back neck
Cast off 4 (5: 5: 6: 7: **6: 7: 8:** 8: 9: 9) sts at beg of next 2 rows. 49 (51: 55: 57: 59: **61: 63: 65:** 69: 71: 75) sts.
Next row (RS): Cast off 4 (5: 5: 6: 7: **6: 7: 8:** 8: 9: 9) sts, patt until there are 8 (8: 10: 10: 10: **11:** 12: 12: 14) sts on right needle and turn, leaving rem sts on a holder.
Work each side of neck separately.
Cast off 4 sts at beg of next row.
Cast off rem 4 (4: 6: 6: 6: **7:** 8: 8: 10) sts.
With RS facing, rejoin yarn to rem sts, cast off centre 25 (**27:** 29) sts, patt to end.
Work to match first side, reversing shapings.

FRONT
Work as given for **front** of laced neck sweater to ★★.
Working in trellis patt throughout, cont straight until 8 (8: 10: 10: 12: **14:** 16) rows less have been worked than on back to start of shoulder shaping, ending with a WS row.

Shape neck
Next row (RS): Patt 20 (22: 24: 26: 28: **28: 30: 32:** 34: 36: 38) sts and turn, leaving rem sts on a holder.
Work each side of neck separately.
Cast off 4 sts at beg of next row.
16 (18: 20: 22: 24: **24: 26: 28:** 30: 32: 34) sts.
Dec 1 st at neck edge of next 4 (3: 3: 2: 2: **3:** 3) rows, then on foll 0 (1: 1: 2: 2: **1:** 2) alt rows.
12 (14: 16: 18: 20: **20: 22: 24:** 25: 27: 29) sts.

Ladies and mens sizes only
Work 3 rows.
Dec 1 st at neck edge of next row. - (**19: 21: 23:** 24: 26: 28) sts.

All sizes
Work 2 (1: 3: 2: 4: **3:** 3) rows, ending with a WS row.
Shape shoulder
Cast off 4 (5: 5: 6: 7: **6: 7: 8:** 8: 9: 9) sts at beg of next and foll alt row.
Work 1 row.
Cast off rem 4 (4: 6: 6: 6: **7:** 8: 8: 10) sts. With RS facing, rejoin yarn to rem sts, cast off centre 17 sts, patt to end.
Work to match first side, reversing shapings.

SLEEVES (both alike)
Work as given for sleeves of laced neck sweater.

MAKING UP
PRESS all pieces as described on the info page.
Laced neck sweater
Join shoulder seams using back stitch, or mattress stitch if preferred.
Collar
With RS facing and 5mm (US 8) needles, slip 8 (**8:** 9) sts from right front holder onto right needle, rejoin yarn and pick up and knit 9 (9: 12: 12: 12: **14:** 16) sts up right side of neck, 27 (**29:** 31) sts from back, 9 (9: 12: 12: 12: **14:** 16) sts down left side of neck, then moss st 8 (**8:** 9) sts from left front holder. 61 (61: 67: 67: 67: **73:** 81) sts.

Row 1 (WS of body, RS of collar): Moss st 8 (**8:** 9) sts, ★K3, P3, rep from ★ to last 11 (**11:** 12) sts, K3, moss st 8 (**8:** 9) sts.
Row 2: Moss st 8 (**8:** 9) sts, ★P3, K3, rep from ★ to last 11 (**11:** 12) sts, P3, moss st 8 (**8:** 9) sts.
Rep these 2 rows for 8 (**11:** 14) cm. Cast off in patt.
Using 2 (**3:** 3) strands of yarn, make a twisted cord approx 100 (**120:** 140) cm long and thread through eyelet holes of front opening. Knot and trim ends as required.

Crew neck sweater
Join right shoulder seam using back stitch, or mattress stitch if preferred.
Neckband
With RS facing and 5mm (US 8) needles, pick up and knit 11 (11: 14: 14: 17: **19:** 21) sts down left side of neck, 17 sts from front, 11 (11: 14: 14: 17: **19:** 21) sts up right side of neck, then 33 (**35:** 37) sts from back. 72 (72: 78: 78: 84: **90:** 96) sts.
Row 1 (WS): ★K3, P3, rep from ★ to end.
Rep this row for 3 cm, ending with a WS row.
Beg with a K row, work in st st for 6 rows. Cast off.
Both sweaters
See information page for finishing instructions, setting in sleeves using the shallow set-in method and, for ladies and mens sizes, leaving side seams open for first 8 cm for side vents.

Chart for yoke

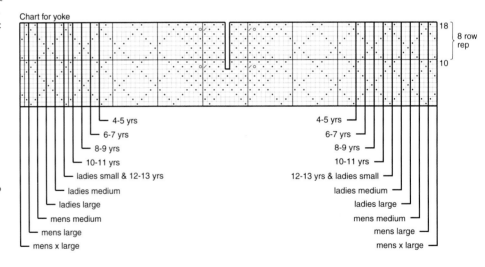

Chart for Trellis pattern

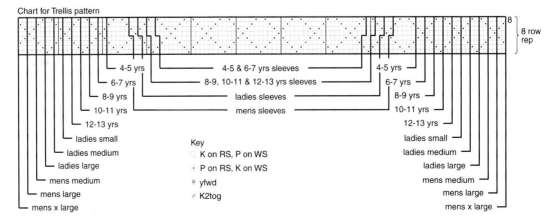

Key
- ☐ K on RS, P on WS
- · P on RS, K on WS
- ○ yfwd
- ╱ K2tog

Elizabeth

Continued from page 25

FRONT

Work as given for back until 10 (10: 10: 12: 12) rows less have been worked to start of shoulder shaping, ending with a WS row.

Shape neck

Next row (RS): Patt 23 (23: 24: 25: 26) sts and turn, leaving rem sts on a holder.

Work each side of neck separately.

Cast off 4 sts at beg of next row.

19 (19: 20: 21: 22) sts.

Dec 1 st at neck edge on next 3 rows, then on foll 2 (2: 2: 3: 3) alt rows.

14 (14: 15: 15: 16) sts.

Work 1 row, ending with a WS row.

Shape shoulder

Cast off 5 sts at beg of next and foll alt row.

Work 1 row.

Cast off rem 4 (4: 5: 5: 6) sts.

With RS facing, rejoin yarn to rem sts, cast off centre 31 (33: 33: 33: 33) sts, patt to end.

Work to match first side, reversing shapings.

SLEEVES (both alike)

Work as given for sleeves of polo neck sweater to ★★★.

Work in bead patt as folls:

Beg with a K row, work in st st for 6 rows.

Row 7 (RS): K1 (1: 2: 3: 3), ★place bead (see beading note), K5, rep from ★ to last 2 (2: 3: 4: 4) sts, place bead, K1 (1: 2: 3: 3).

Beg with a P row, work in st st for 7 rows, inc 1 st at each end of 4th of these rows.

53 (53: 55: 57: 57) sts.

Row 15 (RS): K5 (5: 6: 1: 1), ★place bead (see beading note), K5, rep from ★ to last 6 (6: 7: 2: 2) sts, place bead, K5 (5: 6: 1: 1).

Row 16: Purl.

These 16 rows form bead patt.

Cont in bead patt, shaping sides by inc 1 st at each end of every foll 10th row (from previous inc) to 71 (63: 67: 69: 61) sts, then on every foll 8th row until there are 81 (83: 85: 87: 89) sts.

Complete as given for sleeves of polo neck sweater from ★★★★.

Cardigan

BACK

Cast on 441 (465: 489: 513: 537) sts using 2¾mm (US 2) circular needle and contrast yarn.

Break off contrast yarn and join in main colour.

Complete as given for back of polo neck sweater from ★★.

LEFT FRONT

Cast on 217 (229: 241: 253: 265) sts using 2¾mm (US 2) circular needle and contrast yarn.

Break off contrast yarn and join in main colour.

Row 1 (RS): K1, ★K2, lift first of these 2 sts now on right needle over 2nd st and off right needle, rep from ★ to end.

Row 2: Purl.

Rep rows 1 and 2 once more. 55 (58: 61: 64: 67) sts.

These 4 rows form frill edging.

Change to 3¼mm (US 3) needles.

Beg with a K row, work in st st for 18 (20: 20: 22: 22) rows, ending with a WS row.

Counting in from end of last row, place marker on 27th (29th: 31st: 33rd: 35th) sts in from side seam edge.

Next row (RS) (dec): K2tog, K to within 2 sts of marked st, K2tog, K marked st, K2tog tbl, K to end.

Work 13 rows.

Rep last 14 rows once more and then first of these rows (the dec row) again.

46 (49: 52: 55: 58) sts.

Work 19 rows, ending with a WS row.

Next row (RS) (inc): Inc in first st, K to marker, M1, K marked st, M1, K to end.

Work 17 rows.

Rep last 18 rows once more and then first of these rows (the inc row) again.

55 (58: 61: 64: 67) sts.

Cont straight until left front matches back to beg of armhole shaping, ending with a WS row.

Shape armhole

Cast off 5 (6: 6: 7: 7) sts at beg of next row.

50 (52: 55: 57: 60) sts.

Work 1 row.

Dec 1 st at each end of next 5 (5: 7: 7: 9) rows, then on foll 7 (8: 8: 9: 9) alt rows.

38 (39: 40: 41: 42) sts.

Cont straight until 21 (21: 21: 23: 23) rows less have been worked than on back to start of shoulder shaping, ending with a RS row.

Shape neck

Cast off 8 (9: 9: 9: 9) sts at beg of next row, then 4 sts at beg of foll alt row.

26 (26: 27: 28: 29) sts.

Dec 1 st at neck edge on next 3 rows, then on foll 3 (3: 3: 4: 4) alt rows, then on foll 4th row.

19 (19: 20: 20: 21) sts.

Work 5 rows, ending with a WS row.

Shape shoulder

Cast off 6 (6: 7: 7: 7) sts at beg of next and foll alt row.

Work 1 row.

Cast off rem 7 (7: 6: 6: 7) sts.

RIGHT FRONT

Cast on 217 (229: 241: 253: 265) sts using 2¾mm (US 2) circular needle and contrast yarn.

Break off contrast yarn and join in main colour.

Row 1 (RS): K1, ★K2, lift first of these 2 sts now on right needle over 2nd st and off right needle, rep from ★ to end.

Row 2: Purl.

Rep rows 1 and 2 once more.

55 (58: 61: 64: 67) sts.

These 4 rows form frill edging.

Change to 3¼mm (US 3) needles.

Beg with a K row, work in st st for 18 (20: 20: 22: 22) rows, ending with a WS row.

Counting in from BEG of last row, place marker on 27th (29th: 31st: 33rd: 35th) sts in from side seam edge.

Next row (RS) (dec): K to within 2 sts of marked st, K2tog, K marked st, K2tog tbl, K to last 2 sts, K2tog.

Complete to match left front, reversing shapings.

SLEEVES (both alike)

Cast on 201 (201: 209: 217: 217) sts using 2¾mm (US 2) circular needle and contrast yarn.

Break off contrast yarn and join in main colour.

Complete as given for sleeves of polo neck sweater from ★★.

MAKING UP

PRESS all pieces as described on the info page.

Polo neck sweater

Join right shoulder seam using back stitch, or mattress stitch if preferred.

Collar

With RS facing and 2¾mm (US 2) needles, pick up and knit 26 (26: 26: 28: 28) sts down left side of neck, 23 (25: 25: 25: 25) sts from front, 26 (26: 26: 28: 28) sts up right side of neck, then 39 (41: 41: 43: 43) sts from back. 114 (118: 118: 124: 124) sts.

Beg with a K row, work in st st for 20 cm, ending with a K row.

Beg with a K row, work in rev st st for 4 rows.

Cast off **loosely** knitwise.

Round neck sweater

Join right shoulder seam using back stitch, or mattress stitch if preferred.

Neckband

With RS facing and 2¾mm (US 2) needles, pick up and knit 17 (17: 17: 19: 19) sts down left side of neck, 31 (33: 33: 33: 33) sts from front, 17 (17: 17: 19: 19) sts up right side of neck, then 49 (51: 51: 53: 53) sts from back. 114 (118: 118: 124: 124) sts.

Beg with a K row, work in rev st st for 4 rows.

Cast off **loosely** knitwise (on WS).

Cardigan

Join shoulder seams using back stitch, or mattress stitch if preferred.

Button border

With RS facing, 2¾mm (US 2) needles and contrast yarn, pick up and knit 144 sts along left front opening edge, between neck shaping and cast-on edge.

Beg with a K row, work in rev st st for 4 rows.

Cast off **loosely** knitwise (on WS).

Buttonhole border

Note: Buttonholes are made on the pick up row.

With RS facing, 2¾mm (US 2) needles and contrast yarn, pick up and knit 144 sts along right front opening edge, between cast-on edge and neck shaping, **and at same time** work 9 buttonholes as folls:

Pick up and knit 3 sts, ★pick up and knit **and immediately cast off** 2 sts (this leaves one st on right needle after buttonhole), pick up and knit a further 14 sts, rep from ★ 7 times more, work 1 more buttonhole, then pick up and knit a further 2 sts. (You should have 15 sts between each buttonhole and 3 sts at each end of row beyond end buttonholes.)

Row 1 (WS): Knit to end, working (yfwd) twice over each pair of cast-off sts.

Row 2: Purl, working into front and back of double yfwd of previous row. 144 sts.

Beg with a K row, work in rev st st for 2 rows.

Cast off **loosely** knitwise (on WS).

Neckband

With RS facing, 2¾mm (US 2) needles and contrast yarn, starting and ending level with pick-up row of borders, pick up and knit 37 (38: 38: 40: 40) sts up right side of neck, 39 (41: 41: 43: 43) sts from back, then 37 (38: 38: 40: 40) sts down left side of neck. 113 (117: 117: 123: 123) sts.

Beg with a K row, work in rev st st for 4 rows.

Cast off **loosely** knitwise (on WS).

All versions

See information page for finishing instructions, setting in sleeves using the set-in method.

Tippi

Continued from page 37

MAKING UP
PRESS all pieces as described on the information page.
Sweater
Join right shoulder seam using back stitch, or mattress stitch if preferred.
Collar
With RS facing and 7mm (US 10½) needles, pick up and knit 14 (14: 14: 16: 16) sts down left side of neck, 7 (9: 9: 9: 9) sts from front, 14 (14: 14: 16: 16) sts up right side of neck, then 20 (22: 22: 24: 24) sts from back.
55 (59: 59: 65: 65) sts.
Beg first row with K1, work in rib as given for back for 8 cm.
Change to 8 mm needles and cont in rib until collar measures 12 cm, ending with WS of body (RS of collar) facing for next row.
Next row (WS of body): *K1, P1, M1 purlwise, rep from * to last st, K1. 82 (88: 88: 97: 97) sts.
Next row: P1, *K2, P1, rep from * to end.
Next row: K1, *P2, K1, rep from * to end.
Rep last 2 rows until collar measures 25 cm.
Cast off in rib.
Cardigan
Join shoulder seams using back stitch, or mattress stitch if preferred.
Button border
With RS facing and 7mm (US 10½) needles, pick up and knit 53 sts evenly along left front opening edge, between neck shaping and cast-on edge.
Work in rib as given for back for 4 rows.
Cast off in rib.
Buttonhole border
Work to match button border, picking up sts along right front opening edge and with the addition of 5 buttonholes worked in 2nd row as folls:
Row 2 (RS): Rib 3, *yfwd (to make a buttonhole), K2tog, rib 8, rep from * to end.
Neckband
With RS facing and 7mm (US 10½) needles, starting and ending at cast-off edges of borders, pick up and knit 19 (20: 20: 23: 23) sts up right side of neck, 17 (19: 19: 21: 21) sts from back, then 19 (20: 20: 23: 23) sts down left side of neck.
55 (59: 59: 67: 67) sts.
Work in rib as given for back for 1 row.
Row 2 (RS): Rib 3, yfwd (to make 6th buttonhole), K2tog, rib to end.
Work in rib for a further 2 rows.
Cast off in rib.
Both versions
See information page for finishing instructions, setting in sleeves using the set-in method.

Katie

Continued from page 39

Change to 4mm (US 6) needles.
Beg with a K row, cont in st st as folls:
Work 2 rows.
Next row (RS) (inc): K2, M1, K to last 2 sts, M1, K2.
Working all increases 2 sts in from ends of rows as set by last row, cont as folls:
Cont in st st, inc 1 st at each end of every foll 8th (8th: 8th: 10th: 10th: **10th**) row to 47 (59: 63: 59: 59: **71: 73: 75: 77: 79**) sts, then on every foll 6th (-: -: 8th: 8th: -) row until there are 57 (-: -: 65: 69: **-**) sts.
Cont straight until sleeve measures 29 (33: 37: 41: 43: **47: 47: 47: 48: 48**) cm, ending with a WS row.
Shape top
Cast off 4 (4: 5: 5: 6: **6: 6: 7: 7: 8**) sts at beg of next 2 rows. 49 (51: 53: 55: 57: **59: 61: 61: 63: 63**) sts.
Working all decreases 3 sts in from ends of rows as given for back, dec 2 sts at each end of 7th (5th: 7th: 5th: 7th: **5th: 7th: 5th: 7th: 5th**) and every foll 8th row until 41 (39: 45: 43: 49: **47: 53: 49: 51: 47**) sts rem, then on every foll 4th row until 17 (19: 17: 19: 17: **19: 17: 17: 19: 19**) sts rem.
Work 3 rows, ending with a WS row.
Left sleeve only
Dec 2 sts at each end of next row.
13 (15: 13: 15: 13: **15: 13: 13: 15: 15**) sts.
Cast off 3 (4: 3: 4: 3: **4: 3: 3: 4: 4**) sts at beg of next row, then 5 (6: 5: 6: 5: **6: 5: 5: 6: 6**) sts at beg of foll alt row.
Right sleeve only
Cast off 5 (6: 5: 6: 5: **6: 5: 5: 6: 6**) sts at beg and dec 2 sts at end of next row.
10 (11: 10: 11: 10: **11: 10: 10: 11: 11**) sts.
Work 1 row.
Cast off 5 (6: 5: 6: 5: **6: 5: 5: 6: 6**) sts at beg of next row. Work 1 row.
Both sleeves
Cast off rem 5 sts.

MAKING UP
PRESS all pieces as described on the information page.
Join raglan seams using back stitch, or mattress stitch if preferred.
Collar
Cast on 81 (81: 87: 87: 93: **99: 99: 99: 106: 106**) sts using 3¾mm (US 5) needles.
Childrens sizes only
Row 1 (RS): K3, *P3, K3, rep from * to end.
Row 2: K1, P2, *K3, P3, rep from * to last 6 sts, K3, P2, K1.
Rep last 2 rows until collar measures 8 cm.
Ladies sizes only
Row 1 (RS): K1, P1, *K4, P3, rep from * to last 6 sts, K4, P1, K1.
Row 2: K2, *P4, K3, rep from * to last 6 sts, P4, K2.
These 2 rows set the sts – edge sts worked in garter st with all other sts in rib.
Keeping sts correct as set, cont as folls:
Row 3: Patt 6 sts, M1, rib to last 6 sts, M1, patt 6 sts.
Working all increases as set by last row, inc 1 st at each end of every foll 4th row until there are – (**113: 113: 113: 120: 120**) sts, taking inc sts into rib.
Cont straight until collar measures 10 cm.
All sizes
Cast off in rib.
Sew cast-on edge of collar to neck edge, matching ends of collar to front opening edges.
See information page for finishing instructions, inserting zip into front opening.

Isla

Continued from page 54

Neck border
With RS facing, 2¼mm (US 1) needles and yarn B, work across first 24 sts of left sleeve as folls: K2, K2tog tbl, yfwd, K1, (P3, K3) twice, P3, K1, yfwd, K2tog, K1, K tog last st of left sleeve with first st of front, work across next 41 sts of front as folls: K1, K2tog tbl, yfwd, K1, (P3, K3) 5 times, P3, K1, yfwd, K2tog, K1, K tog last st of front with first st of right sleeve, work across next 23 sts of right sleeve as folls: K1, K2tog tbl, yfwd, K1, (P3, K3) twice, P3, K1, yfwd, K2tog, K1, K tog last st of right sleeve with first st of back, work across rem 42 sts of back as folls: K1, K2tog tbl, yfwd, K1, (P3, K3) 5 times, P3, K1, yfwd, K2tog, K2. 133 sts.
Row 1 (WS): P5, (K3, P3) 5 times, K3, P9, (K3, P3) twice, K3, P9, (K3, P3) 5 times, K3, P9, (K3, P3) twice, K3, P5.
Row 2: *K2, K2tog tbl, yfwd, K1, (P3, K3) twice, P3, K1, yfwd, K2tog, K3, K2tog tbl, yfwd, K1, (P3, K3) 5 times, P3, K1, yfwd, K2tog, K1, rep from * once more, K1.
Rep last 2 rows once more. Cast off in patt.
Cardigan and sweater
See information page for finishing instructions.

DUNOON

Continued from page 44

SLEEVES (both alike)
Cast on 49 (49: 51: 53: 53) sts using 3¼mm (US 3)
needles and yarn A. Knit 2 rows.
Cont in patt foll chart as folls: Work 6 rows.
Change to 4mm (US 6) needles. Work 4 rows.
Inc 1 st at each end of next and every foll 12th (10th:
10th: 10th: 10th) row to 59 (71: 73: 75: 69) sts, then
on every foll 10th (-: -: -: 8th) row until there are
69 (-: -: -: 77) sts, taking inc sts into patt.
Cont straight until sleeve measures 42 (42: 43: 43:
43) cm, ending with a WS row.

Shape top
Keeping patt correct, cast off 3 (4: 4: 5: 5) sts at
beg of next 2 rows. 63 (63: 65: 65: 67) sts.
Dec 1 st at each end of next 3 rows, then on foll
3 alt rows, then on every foll 4th row until
41 (41: 43: 43: 45) sts rem.

Work 1 row, ending with a WS row.
Dec 1 st at each end of next and foll 2 (2: 3: 3: 4)
alt rows, then on foll 3 rows. Cast off rem 29 sts.

MAKING UP
PRESS all pieces as described on the info page.
Join shoulder seams using back stitch, or mattress
stitch if preferred.
Neckband
With RS facing, 3¼mm (US 3) needles and yarn
A, pick up and knit 30 (31: 31: 33: 33) sts up right
side of neck, 33 (35: 35: 37: 37) sts from back, then
30 (31: 31: 33: 33) sts down left side of neck.
93 (97: 97: 103: 103) sts.
Knit 2 rows. Cast off knitwise (on WS).
Button border
With RS facing, 3¼mm (US 3) needles and yarn

A, pick up and knit 101 sts evenly along left front
opening edge, between top of neckband and
cast-on edge.
Knit 2 rows. Cast off knitwise (on WS).
Buttonhole border
Work to match button border, picking up sts along
right front opening edge and with the addition
of 8 buttonholes worked in row 2 as folls:-
Row 2 (RS): ★K10, K2tog, yfwd, rep from ★ 7
times more, K5.
Fringe
Using colours to match knitting, cut 7 cm
lengths of yarn and knot pairs of these threads
through each stitch around lower edge of body.
Trim fringe to 3 cm.
See information page for finishing instructions,
setting in sleeves using the set-in method.

DENNY

Continued from page 47

SLEEVES (both alike)
Cast on 63 (63: 65: 67: 67) sts using 2¾mm (US 2)
needles and yarn A.
Work in moss st as given for back for 5 rows,
ending with a RS row.
Join in yarn B.
Row 6 (WS): Using yarn B P1, ★using yarn A
P1, using yarn B P1, rep from ★ to end.
Break off yarn B.
Work in moss st for a further 5 rows.
Row 12 (WS) (inc): P3 (3: 2: 3: 3), ★M1, P7 (7: 6:
5: 5), rep from ★ to last 4 (4: 3: 4: 4) sts, M1, P4 (4:
3: 4: 4).
72 (72: 76: 80: 80) sts.
Change to 3¼mm (US 3) needles.
Join in yarn B.
Starting and ending rows as indicated, repeating
the 4 st pattern repeat 18 (18: 19: 20: 20) times
across rows and repeating the 4 row repeat
throughout, cont in patt foll chart as folls:
Inc 1 st at each end of 9th (7th: 9th: 9th: 7th) and
every foll 8th (6th: 6th: 6th: 6th) row to 82 (106:
112: 116: 110) sts, then on every foll 6th (4th: -: -:
4th) row until there are 104 (108: -: -: 120) sts,
taking inc sts into patt.
Cont straight until sleeve measures 42 (42: 43: 43:
43) cm, ending with a WS row.

Shape top
Keeping patt correct, cast off 5 (6: 6: 7: 7) sts at
beg of next 2 rows. 94 (96: 100: 102: 106) sts.
Dec 1 st at each end of next 7 rows, then on foll
4 alt rows, then on every foll 4th row until 66
(68: 74: 76: 82) sts rem.
Work 1 row, ending with a WS row.
Dec 1 st at each end of next and foll 3 (4: 7: 8: 11)
alt rows, then on foll 7 rows. 44 sts.
Cast off 5 sts at beg of next 2 rows.
Cast off rem 34 sts.

MAKING UP
PRESS all pieces as described on the info page.
Join shoulder seams using back stitch, or mattress
stitch if preferred.
Button border
Slip 9 sts left on left front holder onto 2¾mm
(US 2) needles and rejoin yarn A with RS facing.
Cont in moss st as set until border, when slightly
stretched, fits up left front opening edge to neck
shaping, ending with a WS row.
Cast off in moss st. Slip st border in place.
Mark positions for 7 buttons on this border –
first to come in first row of border, last to come
1.5 cm down from neck shaping and rem 5
buttons evenly spaced between.

Buttonhole border
Work to match button border, rejoining yarn with
WS facing and with the addition of 7 buttonholes
worked to correspond with positions marked for
buttons as folls:
Next row (buttonhole row) (RS): Moss st 4 sts,
yrn, work 2 tog, moss st 3 sts.
When border is complete, ending with a WS
row, cast off in moss st.
Slip st border in place.
Collar
Cast on 97 (99: 99: 107: 107) sts using 2¾mm (US 2)
needles and yarn A.
Work in moss st as given for back for 5 rows,
ending with a RS row.
Join in yarn B.
Row 6 (WS): Using yarn A (K1, P1) twice, using
yarn B P1, ★using yarn A P1, using yarn B P1, rep
from ★ to last 4 sts, using yarn A (P1, K1) twice.
Break off yarn B.
Work in moss st for a further 32 rows.
Cast off in moss st.
Sew cast-off edge of collar to neck edge,
positioning ends of collar halfway across top of
borders.
See information page for finishing instructions,
setting in sleeves using the set-in method.

SPENCER

Continued from page 49

MAKING UP
PRESS all pieces as described on the
information page.
Join right shoulder seam using back stitch, or
mattress stitch if preferred.

Neckband
With RS facing, 3¼mm (US 3) needles and yarn A,
pick up and knit 17 (**20**) sts down left side of neck,
17 (17: 19: **21: 21: 23**) sts from front, 17 (**20**) sts
up right side of neck, then 33 (33: 35: **39: 39: 41**) sts

from back. 84 (84: 88: **100: 100: 104**) sts.
Row 1 (WS): ★K2, P2, rep from ★ to end.
Rep this row for 6 (**7**) cm. Cast off in rib.
See information page for finishing instructions,
setting in sleeves using the set-in method.

CALUM

Continued from page 59

Insert zip into front opening.
See info page for finishing instructions.

Jacket

Join raglan seams using back stitch, or mattress stitch if preferred.

Collar

With RS facing and 5mm (US 8) needles, beg and ending at front opening edge, pick up and knit 17 (17: 19: 19: 19) sts up right side of neck, 9 sts from right sleeve, 22 (22: 25: 25: 25) sts from back, 9 sts from left sleeve, then 17 (17: 19: 19: 19) sts down left side of neck. 74 (74: 81: 81: 81) sts.

Row 1: K1, P3, *K3, P4, rep from * to last 7 sts, K3, P3, K1.

Row 2: K4, *P3, K4, rep from * to end.
Rep last 2 rows until collar measures 16 cm.
Cast off in rib.
Positioning top of zip 8 cm above neck edge, insert zip into front opening. Fold collar in half to inside and loosely stitch in place. See information page for finishing instructions.

BETH

Continued from page 62

SLEEVES (both alike)
Cast on 66 (66: 66: 70: 70) sts using 2¼mm (US 1) needles and yarn A.
Work in rib as given for back for 14 (12: 12: 14: 12) rows.
Inc 1 st at each end of next and foll 14th (12th: 12th: 14th: 12th) row. 70 (70: 70: 74: 74) sts.
Work in rib for a further 5 (9: 9: 5: 9) rows, dec (dec: inc: dec: dec) 1 st at centre of last row. 69 (69: 71: 73: 73) sts.
Break off yarn A and join in yarn B.
Change to 3mm (US 2/3) needles.
Beg with a K row, cont in st st, as folls:
Work 8 (2: 2: 6: 2) rows.
Next row (RS) (inc): K3, M1, K to last 3 sts, M1, K3.
Working all increases 3 sts in from ends of rows as set by last row, inc 1 st at each end of every foll 14th (12th: 12th: 12th: 12th) row to 77 (91: 93: 95: 89) sts, then on every foll 12th (-: -: -: 10th) row until there are 89 (-: -: -: 97) sts.
Cont straight until sleeve measures 44 (44: 44: 45: 45) cm, ending with a WS row.

Shape top
Cast off 4 (4: 4: 6: 6) sts at beg of next 2 rows.
81 (83: 85: 83: 85) sts.
Dec 1 st at each end of next 5 rows, then on foll 3 alt rows, then on every foll 4th row until 49 (51: 53: 47: 49) sts rem.
Work 1 row, ending with a WS row.
Dec 1 st at each end of next and foll 1 (2: 3: 0: 1) alt rows, then on foll 3 rows. 39 sts.
Cast off 4 sts at beg of next 2 rows.
Cast off rem 31 sts.

MAKING UP
PRESS all pieces as described on the information page.
Join shoulder seams using back stitch, or mattress stitch if preferred.

Button border
Slip 6 sts from left front holder onto 2¼mm (US 1) needles and rejoin yarn B with RS facing.
Cont in moss st until border, when slightly stretched, fits up left front opening edge to neck shaping, ending with a WS row.
Break yarn and leave sts on a holder.
Slip stitch border in place.
Mark positions for 9 buttons on this border – lowest 2 level with buttonholes already worked in right front, top button to come just above neck shaping and rem 6 buttons evenly spaced between.

Buttonhole border
Slip 6 sts from right front holder onto 2¼mm (US 1) needles and rejoin yarn B with WS facing.
Cont in moss st until border, when slightly stretched, fits up right front opening edge to neck shaping, ending with a WS row and with the addition of a further 6 buttonholes worked to correspond with positions marked on left front for buttons as folls:
Buttonhole row (RS): Moss st 3 sts, yrn (to make a buttonhole), work 2 tog, moss st 1 st.
When border is required length, ending with a WS row, do NOT break yarn.
Slip stitch border in place.

Neckband
With RS facing, 2¼mm (US 1) and yarn B, moss st across 6 sts of buttonhole border, pick up and knit 44 (45: 45: 48: 48) sts up right side of neck, 43 (45: 45: 47: 47) sts from back, and 44 (45: 45: 48: 48) sts down left side of neck, then moss st across 6 sts of button border.
143 (147: 147: 155: 155) sts.
Work in moss st as set by borders for 3 rows.
Row 4 (RS): Moss st 3 sts, yrn (to make 9th buttonhole), work 2 tog, moss st to end.
Work in moss st for a further 4 rows.
Cast off in moss st (on WS).
See information page for finishing instructions, setting in sleeves using the set-in method.

SALEN

Continued from page 72

Shape top
Cast off 3 (4: 4: 5: 5) sts at beg of next 2 rows.
70 (70: 72: 72: 74) sts.
Dec 1 st at each end of next 3 rows, then on foll 3 alt rows, then on every foll 4th row until 48 (48: 50: 50: 52) sts rem.
Work 1 row, ending with a WS row.
Dec 1 st at each end of next and foll 2 (2: 3: 3: 4) alt rows, then on foll 5 rows. 32 sts.
Cast off 4 sts at beg of next 2 rows. Cast off rem 24 sts.

MAKING UP
PRESS all pieces as described on the info page.
Join shoulder seams using back stitch, or mattress stitch if preferred.

Neckband
With RS facing and 3¼mm (US 3) needles, slip 24 (25: 25: 25: 25) sts from right front holder onto right needle, rejoin yarn A and pick up and knit 23 (23: 23: 25: 25) sts up right side of neck, 35 (37: 37: 39: 39) sts from back, and 23 (23: 23: 25: 25) sts down left side of neck, then patt across 24 (25: 25: 25: 25) sts from left front holder as folls: using yarn A K7 (8: 8: 8: 8), using second ball of yarn B patt 17 sts. 129 (133: 133: 139: 139) sts.
Row 1 (WS): Using yarn B patt 17 sts, using yarn A K1, *P1, K1, rep from * to last 17 sts, using yarn B patt 17 sts.
Rep this row 3 times more.
Cast off in patt.
Fold front opening edges to inside along line of slipped sts and sew in place. Attach top half of stud fasteners to right front facing (on inside), spacing them centrally across and evenly along facing. Attach other half of stud fasteners to outside of left front to correspond, so that front borders overlap.
See information page for finishing instructions, setting in sleeves using the set-in method.

NEVIS

Continued from page 69

Shape neck
Dec 1 st at raglan edge of next 1 (1: 1: 1: 3) rows, then on foll 5 (2: 5: 2: 4) alt rows **and at same time** dec 1 st at neck edge of next and foll 6th (0: 6th: 0: 6th) row. 11 (17: 14: 20: 17) sts.
Work 1 row, ending with a WS row.
Dec 1 st at raglan edge of next and foll 5 (9: 7: 11: 9) alt rows **and at same time** dec 1 st at neck edge of next and every foll 4th row. 2 sts.
Next row (WS): P2.
Next row: K2tog and fasten off.

RIGHT FRONT
Cast on 24 (26: 28: 30: 32) sts using 7mm (US 10½) needles and yarn B.
Work in garter st for 6 rows, ending with a WS row.
Change to 8mm (US 11) needles.
Starting and ending rows as indicated, work in patt foll chart for lower edge as folls:
Work 2 rows.
Dec 1 st at end of next row. 23 (25: 27: 29: 31) sts.
Work rem 2 rows of lower edge chart, ending with a RS row.
Beg with a P row, cont in st st using yarn A only as folls:
Work 3 rows, ending with a WS row.
Dec 1 st at end of next and every foll 6th row until 19 (21: 23: 25: 27) sts rem.
Complete to match left front, reversing shapings.

SLEEVES
Cast on 33 (33: 33: 35: 35) sts using 7mm (US 10½) needles and yarn B.
Work in garter st for 6 rows, ending with a WS row.
Change to 8mm (US 11) needles.
Starting and ending rows as indicated, work in patt foll chart for lower edge as folls:

Work 4 rows.
Inc 1 st at each end of next row.
35 (35: 35: 37: 37) sts.
Beg with a P row, cont in st st using yarn A only as folls:
Inc 1 st at each end of every foll 12th (10th: 10th: 10th: 8th) row to 45 (47: 43: 45: 53) sts, then on every foll – (-: 8th: 8th: -) row until there are – (-: 49: 51: -) sts.
Cont straight until sleeve measures 48 (48: 49: 49: 49) cm, ending with a WS row.
Starting and ending rows as indicated, work in patt foll chart for yoke as folls:
Work 2 rows, ending with a WS row.
Shape raglans
Keeping chart correct as set until all 20 rows have been worked and then completing sleeve in st st using yarn A, cont as folls:
Cast off 4 sts at beg of next 2 rows.
37 (39: 41: 43: 45) sts.
Dec 1 st at each end of next and every foll alt row until 11 sts rem.
Work 1 row, ending with a WS row.
Left sleeve only
Dec 1 st at each end of next row. 9 sts.
Cast off 2 sts at beg of next row. 7 sts.
Dec 1 st at beg of next row. 6 sts.
Cast off 3 sts at beg of next row. 3 sts.
Right sleeve only
Cast off 3 sts at beg and dec 1 st at end of next row.
Work 1 row.
Rep last 2 rows once more. 3 sts.
Both sleeves
Cast off rem 3 sts.

MAKING UP
PRESS all pieces as described on the info page.
Join raglan seams using back stitch, or mattress stitch if preferred.

Button border and left collar
Cast on 5 sts using 7mm (US 10½) needles and yarn A.
Work in garter st until border, when slightly stretched, fits up left front opening edge to start of front slope shaping, sewing in place as you go along and ending at inner (attached) edge.
Shape for collar
Cont in garter st, inc 1 st at beg of next and every foll alt row until there are 21 sts.
Cont straight until collar, **unstretched,** fits up front slope, across top of sleeve and across to centre back neck, sewing in place as you go along and ending at outer (free) edge.
Next row: K14, slip next st onto right needle, bring yarn to front of work between needles and slip same st back onto left needle, turn and K to end.
Next row: K7, slip next st onto right needle, bring yarn to front of work between needles and slip same st back onto left needle, turn and K to end.
Cast off all 21 sts, working the wrapped loop and the st it wraps tog.
Mark positions of 5 buttons on button border – first to come 10 cm up from cast-on edge, last to come just below start of neck shaping and rem 3 buttons evenly spaced between.
Buttonhole border
Work to match button border, with the addition of 5 buttonholes to correspond with positions marked for buttons worked as folls:
Buttonhole row (RS): K2, yfwd, K2tog, K1.
Join back neck seam of collar sections. See information page for finishing instructions.

One colour cardigan
Work exactly as given for fairisle cardigan but using same colour yarn throughout.

THISTLE

Continued from page 65

Upper right front
Cast on 44 (46: 48: 50: 52) sts using 5½mm (US 9) needles.
Remembering to make buttonholes as required, work in moss st as given for lower right front until upper right front measures 11 cm, ending with a RS row.
Shape raglan armhole
Cast off 4 sts at beg of next row.
40 (42: 44: 46: 48) sts.
Complete to match upper left front, reversing shapings.

SLEEVES
Cast on 39 (39: 41: 43: 43) sts using 5mm (US 8) needles.
Work in moss st as given for back for 10 rows, ending with a WS row.
Change to 5½mm (US 9) needles.
Cont in moss st, inc 1 st at each end of next and every foll 12th (10th: 10th: 10th: 10th) row to

43 (55: 59: 61: 53) sts, then on every foll 10th (8th: 8th: 8th: 8th) row until there are 59 (61: 63: 65: 67) sts, taking inc sts into moss st.
Cont straight until sleeve measures 45 (45: 46: 46: 46) cm, ending with a WS row.
Shape raglan
Cast off 4 sts at beg of next 2 rows.
51 (53: 55: 57: 59) sts.
Dec 1 st at each end of next and every foll 4th row to 39 (41: 43: 45: 47) sts, then on every foll alt row until 11 sts rem.
Work 1 row, ending with a WS row.
Left sleeve only
Dec 1 st at each end of next row. 9 sts.
Cast off 2 sts at beg of next row. 7 sts.
Dec 1 st at beg of next row. 6 sts.
Cast off 3 sts at beg of next row. 3 sts.
Right sleeve only
Cast off 3 sts at beg and dec 1 st at end of next row.
Work 1 row.
Rep last 2 rows once more. 3 sts.

Both sleeves
Cast off rem 3 sts.

MAKING UP
PRESS all pieces as described on the info page.
Join raglan seams using back stitch, or mattress stitch if preferred. Join lower back and right front to upper back and right front in same way as for left front sections.
Collar
With RS facing and 5mm (US 8) needles, starting and ending 7 sts in from front opening edge, pick up and knit 13 (14: 14: 16: 16) sts up right side of neck, 9 sts from right sleeve, 17 (19: 19: 21: 21) sts from back, 9 sts from left sleeve, then 13 (14: 14: 16: 16) sts down left side of neck.
61 (65: 65: 71: 71) sts.
Work in moss st as given for back for 13 cm.
Cast off in moss st.
Fold collar in half to inside and stitch in place.
See information page for finishing instructions.

INFORMATION PAGE

TENSION

Obtaining the correct tension is perhaps the single factor which can make the difference between a successful garment and a disastrous one. It controls both the shape and size of an article, so any variation, however slight, can distort the finished look of the garment.

We recommend that you knit a square in pattern and/or stocking stitch (depending on the pattern instructions) of perhaps 5 - 10 more stitches and 5 - 10 more rows than those given in the tension note. Press the finished square under a damp cloth and mark out the central 10cm square with pins. If you have too many stitches to 10cm try again using thicker needles, if you have too few stitches to 10cm try again using finer needles. Once you have achieved the correct tension your garment will be knitted to the measurements indicated in the size diagram shown at the end of the pattern.

SIZING AND SIZE DIAGRAM NOTE

The instructions are given for the smallest size. Where they vary, work the figures in brackets for the larger sizes. **One set of figures refers to all sizes**.

Included with every pattern in this magazine is a 'size diagram', or sketch of the finished garment and its dimensions. The purpose of this is to enable you to accurately achieve a perfect fitting garment without the need for worry during knitting. The size diagram shows the finished width of the garment at the under-arm point, and it is this measurement that the knitter should choose first; a useful tip is to measure one of your own garments which is a comfortable fit. Having chosen a size based on width, look at the corresponding length for that size; if you are not happy with the total length which we recommend, adjust your own garment before beginning your armhole shaping - any adjustment after this point will mean that your sleeve will not fit into your garment easily - don't forget to take your adjustment into account if there is any side seam shaping. Finally, look at the sleeve length; the size diagram shows the finished sleeve measurement, taking into account any top-arm insertion length. Measure your body between the centre of your neck and your wrist, this measurement should correspond to half the garment width plus the sleeve length. Again, your sleeve length may be adjusted, but remember to take into consideration your sleeve increases if you do adjust the length - you must increase more frequently than the pattern states to shorten your sleeve, less frequently to lengthen it.

CHART NOTE

Many of the patterns in the book are worked from charts. Each square on a chart represents a stitch and each line of squares a row of knitting.

Each colour used is given a different symbol or letter and these are shown in the **materials** section, or in the **key** alongside the chart of each pattern. When working from the charts, read odd rows (K) from right to left and even rows (P) from left to right, unless otherwise stated.

KNITTING WITH COLOUR

There are two main methods of working colour into a knitted fabric: **Intarsia** and **Fairisle** techniques. The first method produces a single thickness of fabric and is usually used where a colour is only required in a particular area of a row and does not form a repeating pattern across the row, as in the fairisle technique.

Intarsia: Cut short lengths of yarn for each motif or block of colour used in a row. Joining in the various colours at the appropriate point on the row, link one colour to the next by twisting them around each other where they meet on the wrong side to avoid gaps.

Fairisle type knitting: When two or three colours are worked repeatedly across a row, strand the yarn **not** in use loosely behind the stitches being worked. It is advisable not to carry the stranded or "floating" yarns over more than three stitches at a time, but to weave them under and over the colour you are working. The "floating" yarns are therefore caught at the back of the work.

FINISHING INSTRUCTIONS

After working for hours knitting a garment, it seems a great pity that many garments are spoiled because such little care is taken in the pressing and finishing process. Follow the following tips for a truly professional-looking garment.

Pressing

Darn in all ends neatly along the selvage edge or a colour join, as appropriate.

Block out each piece of knitting using pins and gently press each piece, omitting the ribs, using a warm iron over a damp cloth. **Tip:** Take special care to press the edges, as this will make sewing up both easier and neater.

Stitching

When stitching the pieces together, remember to match areas of colour and texture very carefully where they meet.

Use a seam stitch such as back stitch or mattress stitch for all main knitting seams, and join all ribs and neckband with a flat seam unless otherwise stated.

Construction

Having completed the pattern instructions, join left shoulder and neckband seams as detailed above. Sew the top of the sleeve to the body of the garment using the method detailed in the pattern, referring to the appropriate guide:

Square set-in sleeves: Set sleeve head into armhole, the straight sides at top of sleeve to form a neat right-angle to cast-off sts at armhole on back and front.

Shallow set-in sleeves: Join cast-off sts at beg of armhole shaping to cast-off sts at start of sleeve-head shaping. Sew sleeve head into armhole, easing in shapings.

Set-in sleeves: Set in sleeve, easing sleeve head into armhole.

Join side and sleeve seams.
Slip stitch pocket edgings and linings into place.
Sew on buttons to correspond with buttonholes.
After sewing up, press seams and hems.
Ribbed welts and neckbands and any areas of garter stitch should not be pressed.

 = Easy, straight forward knitting

 = Suitable for the average knitter

 = For the more experienced knitter

ABBREVIATIONS

K	knit
P	purl
st(s)	stitch(es)
inc	increas(e)(ing)
dec	decreas(e)(ing)
st st	stocking stitch (1 row K, 1 row P)
garter st	garter stitch (K every row)
beg	begin(ning)
foll	following
rem	remain(ing)
rev	revers(e)(ing)
rep	repeat
alt	alternate
cont	continue
patt	pattern
tog	together
mm	millimetres
cm	centimetres
in(s)	inch(es)
RS	right side
WS	wrong side
sl1	slip one sticth
psso	pass slipped stitch over
p2sso	pass 2 slipped stitches over
tbl	through back of loop
M1	make one stitch by picking up horizontal loop before next stitch and knitting into back of it
yfwd	yarn forward
yrn	yarn round needle
yon	yarn over needle
cn	cable needle

STOCKIST INFORMATION

For details of U.K. stockists or any other information concerning this book please contact:

Rowan Yarns
Green Lane Mill
Holmfirth
West Yorkshire
HD9 2DX

Tel: +44 (0)1484 681881
Fax: +44 (0)1484 687920
Email: seasons@knitrowan.com
www.knitrowan.com

ROWAN OVERSEAS DISTRIBUTORS

BELGIUM
Pavan
Koningin Astridlaan 78
B9000 Gent
Tel: (32) 9 221 8591

CANADA
Diamond Yarn
9697 St Laurent
Montreal
Quebec
H3L 2N1
Tel: (514) 388 6188
www.diamondyarns.com

Diamond Yarn (Toronto)
155 Martin Ross
Unit 3
Toronto
Ontario
M3J 2L9
Tel: (416) 736 6111
www.diamondyarns.com

DENMARK
Individual stockists
- please contact
Rowan for details

FRANCE
Elle Tricot
8 Rue du Coq
67000 Strasbourg
Tel: (33) 3 88 23 03 13
www.elletricote.com

GERMANY
Wolle & Design
Wolfshovener Strasse 76
52428 Julich-Stetternich
Tel : (49) 2461 54735.
www.wolleundesign.de

HOLLAND
de Afstap
Oude Leliestraat 12
1015 AW Amsterdam
Tel : (31) 20 6231445

HONG KONG
East Unity Co Ltd
Room 902,
Block A
Kailey Industrial Centre
12 Fung Yip Street
Chai Wan
Tel : (852) 2869 7110.

ICELAND
Storkurinn
Kjorgardi
Laugavegi 59
Reykjavik
Tel: (354) 551 82 58

JAPAN
DiaKeito Co Ltd
2-3-11 Senba-Higashi
Minoh City
Osaka
Tel : (81) 727 27 6604
www.rowanintl-jp.com

NORWAY
Hera
Tennisun 3D
0777 OSLO
Tel: (47) 22 49 54 65

SWEDEN
Wincent
Norrtulsgaten 65
11345 Stockholm
Tel: (46) 8 673 70 60

U.S.A.
Rowan USA
5 Northern Boulevard
Amherst
New Hampshire 03031
Tel: (1 603) 886 5041/5043